Effective Performance Management

Effective Performance Management

SHEILA J. COSTELLO

The Business Skills Express Series

BUSINESS ONE IRWIN/MIRROR PRESS
Burr Ridge, Illinois
New York, New York
Boston, Massachusetts

© RICHARD D. IRWIN, INC., 1994

Mirror Press: David R. Helmstadter
                       Carla F. Tishler

Editor-in-Chief: Jeffrey A. Krames
Project editor: Mary Vandercar
Production manager: Bob Lange
Interior designer: Jeanne M. Rivera
Cover designer: Tim Kaage
Art coordinator: Heather Burbridge
Illustrator: Boston Graphics, Inc.
Compositor: Alexander Typesetting, Inc.
Typeface: 12/14 Criterion
Printer: Malloy Lithographing, Inc.

Library of Congress Cataloging-in-Publication Data

Costello, Sheila J.
    Effective performance management / Sheila J. Costello.
       p.   cm. — (Business skills express series)
    ISBN 1-55623-867-3
    1. Employees—Rating of.   2. Performance—Management.   I. Title.
II. Series.
    HF5549.5.R3C63   1994
    658.3'125—dc20   93–21873

Printed in the United States of America
    2 3 4 5 6 7 8 9 0 ML 0 9 8 7 6 5 4 3

PREFACE

Managing performance in the workplace involves letting employees know what is expected of them, how they are doing, and how they can do an even better job. Only then can employees contribute their best, use their abilities to the fullest, and feel connected to their organization.

As a supervisor or manager, one of your most important responsibilities to your organization is to manage performance well. You need to manage not only your own performance but also the performance of the many individuals you will supervise and develop over the years. Your ability to manage performance effectively will contribute to your organization's success and will positively affect the people who work within your organization.

Managing performance does not have to be a difficult task. As you read through this book and complete the exercises, you will soon become educated in the three areas of performance management:

- Performance and development planning.
- Interim coaching and progress reviews.
- Performance appraisals and development reviews.

This book's step-by-step approach will help you develop all the skills necessary to build and maintain peak performance in the workplace. So relax, enjoy, and learn.

Sheila J. Costello

ABOUT THE AUTHOR

Sheila J. Costello is a private consultant specializing in management training and development. Ms. Costello's professional training and consulting experience includes positions as national Director of Training and Development for American Mutual Insurance Companies, Manager of Training for AtlantiCare Medical Center Corporation, Regional Program Director for International Training Corporation, Director for the Center for Business and Industry at Massachusetts Bay Community College, Program Director for the Bentley College Center for Continuing and Professional Education, and Unit Coordinator for Boston Head Start Programs. She continues to serve as an adjunct faculty member for several private and public colleges and associations, training business professionals in a variety of management skills. Ms. Costello is committed to providing practical rather than theoretical information to address many of today's management concerns.

About Business One Irwin

Business One Irwin is the nation's premier publisher of business books. As a Times Mirror company, we work closely with Times Mirror training organizations, including Zenger-Miller, Inc., Learning International, Inc., and Kaset International to serve the training needs of business and industry.

About the Business Skills Express Series

This expanding series of authoritative, concise and fast-paced books delivers high quality training on key business topics at a remarkably affordable cost. The series will help managers, supervisors, and front line personnel in organizations of all sizes and types hone their business skills while enhancing job performance and career satisfaction.

Business Skills Express books are ideal for employee seminars, independent self-study, on-the-job training and classroom-based instruction. Express books are also convenient-to-use references at work.

CONTENTS

Self-Assessment

As a way of assessing how much you already know and are using in your performance management process, complete this simple self-assessment. It may confirm your confidence in your abilities to manage performance or it may suggest areas where improvements can be made. In either case, it will provide you with a starting point as you explore *Effective Performance Management*.

	Almost Always	Sometimes	Almost Never
1. I clearly understand my company's goals and objectives.	————	————	————
2. I clearly understand my division's or department's goals and objectives.	————	————	————
3. I clearly understand my own goals and objectives.	————	————	————
4. I have a written performance plan, outlining annual goals and objectives for my own performance.	————	————	————
5. I receive performance plan updates whenever changes occur in company goals or directions that alter my plan.	————	————	————
6. I regularly communicate overall company, division, and department goals to all of my employees.	————	————	————
7. I involve my employees in establishing their own performance goals and objectives each year.	————	————	————
8. I conduct annual performance planning meetings with each of my employees at the start of his or her performance cycle.	————	————	————
9. I provide written copies of annual performance goals and objectives for each of my employees.	————	————	————
10. I provide ongoing feedback and coaching to each of my employees throughout the year.	————	————	————
11. I praise all of my employees for good performance in a timely and constructive way.	————	————	————

continued

	Almost Always	Sometimes	Almost Never
12. I reprimand all of my employees for poor performance in a timely and constructive way.	_____	_____	_____
13. I meet with each of my employees quarterly to review his or her performance against his or her goals and objectives.	_____	_____	_____
14. I hold annual performance review meetings with each employee to discuss his or her yearly progress against his or her overall performance plan.	_____	_____	_____
15. I provide written annual performance appraisals and development reviews for each of my employees.	_____	_____	_____

1 | An Introduction

This chapter will help you to:

- Define effective performance management.
- See why performance management is essential.
- Understand how a performance management system works.

It was Nancy MacDonald's first day on the job. She was excited about her new position as a customer service supervisor at United International Bank. She looked forward to attending the bank's orientation and meeting with her new boss, William Weatherby, the director of customer service. She arrived at the bank at 7:45 A.M. all fired up and raring to go. From 8 A.M. to 10 A.M. she attended the standard bank orientation, which consisted of a warm welcome and an opportunity to sign up for benefits. Nothing about the bank's culture, goals, or expectations was communicated; but Nancy left the orientation with a smile on her face, knowing that her boss would provide her with the missing information.

As directed by the department secretary, Nancy reported to William Weatherby's office at 10 A.M. for a meeting. She assumed he was eager to discuss performance expectations and to get her started on her work. After sitting in his empty office for 30 minutes, she decided to get up and ask the secretary where he might be. The secretary did not know where he was, but she suggested that Nancy could wait in the waiting room for him. With no office, no paperwork to review, and no projects to start on, Nancy sat alone in the waiting room feeling extremely isolated and wondering what she should do. At noon she stuck her head out to ask where the lunchroom was and informed the secretary that she was going to take a quick lunch.

Following lunch, she dutifully reported back to her secretary and reminded her that, if William Weatherby was looking for her, she would be in the waiting room. She sat there, uninterrupted, until 2 P.M. At that time the secretary popped her head in and said, ''I just got a call from Mr. Weatherby, and he said he's tied up and doesn't think he'll be able to meet with you today.'' After delivering her announcement, the secretary promptly left. Nancy was left with nothing to do.

Weeks passed and Nancy made many attempts to meet with her boss about her new job. Five meetings were canceled; and now, a month later, Nancy is still wondering where William Weatherby is. ■

■ Questions to Consider

1. What went wrong? _____

   _____

   _____

2. How do you think Nancy feels about her situation? _____

   _____

   _____

3. How might Nancy's feelings affect her work performance both in the short term and in the long term?

Short-term impact: _____

_____

Long-term impact: _____

_____

4. If you were Nancy's manager, what might you have done differently?

_____

_____

_____

WHAT IS PERFORMANCE MANAGEMENT?

Just as a solid foundation is critical to building and supporting a home, a solid performance management plan is essential to developing an organization and the people within it. An effective performance management system should serve as the cornerstone and driving force behind all organizational decisions, work efforts, and resource allocations.

Performance management supports a company's or organization's overall business goals by linking the work of each individual employee or manager to the overall mission of the work unit. Generally, this is accomplished by establishing individual goals and objectives that are tied directly to the organization's purpose or direction. An effective performance management process generally starts with identifying clear goals, which are used as the foundation for ongoing coaching and performance review.

Performance management involves:

- Analyzing the objectives and goals for your department or work unit and ensuring that they relate to the overall goals of your company or organization.
- Analyzing your employee's skills and assignments as they relate to company, department, or unit goals.
- Clearly communicating performance goals and expectations to each employee and gaining agreement on those goals and expectations.

- Recognizing and acknowledging the good performance of employees.

- Recognizing where performance needs to be improved and providing employees with the necessary support to improve it.

The cascading diagram shown in Figure 1.1 depicts the interrelationship among various organization levels. This interrelationship is critical to the accomplishment of organization goals and objectives.

FIGURE 1.1   INTERRELATIONSHIP AMONG ORGANIZATION LEVELS

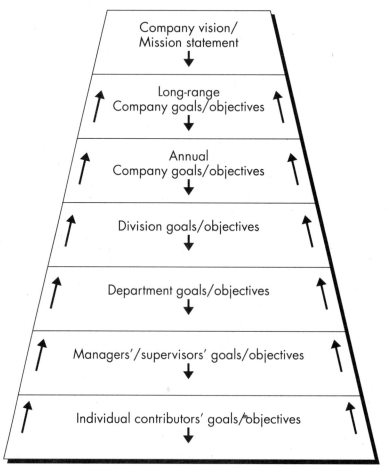

Goals are statements of general direction or intent. They are broad, timeless, and unconcerned with particular achievement within a specific time period. Goals are aspirations. **"To create winning customer relationships"** is a goal.

Objectives are specific statements that describe results to be achieved, when, and by whom, for a goal to be accomplished. They are quantifiable, observable achievements that can be measured. They should be clearly differentiated from the activitives required to attain them. Objectives are expectations. **"To return customer calls within 24 hours of their receipt throughout this fiscal year"** is an objective.

Every objective should relate to a goal and to the overall mission of the organization.

■ Exercise 1.1

All performance objectives should be correlated to the overall mission of your organization. Take a few minutes to respond to the following questions. You may not be able to answer all of them fully at this time, but you will become aware of those areas where further attention is needed to establish and implement an effective performance management system.

1. What is the overall mission or vision of your organization?

_____

_____

2. What are the long-term goals and objectives of your organization?

_____

_____

3. What are the short-term or annual goals and objectives of your organization?

_____

_____

4. What are your division's or department's goals and objectives?

_____

_____

5. What are your work unit's goals and objectives?

_____

_____

6. What are your individual work goals and objectives?

_____

_____

7. What are the goals and objectives of the employees who report to you, if applicable?

_____

_____

Review your responses to the questions in Exercise 1.1. If you were unable to answer any of the questions, you may want to seek further information from others in your organization. To do this, start by asking your manager, and then move up the organization ladder until you can answer all questions to your satisfaction. Look carefully at the goals and objectives you have written for each question. They should correlate with the vision and overall goals and objectives of your organization.

WHY IS PERFORMANCE MANAGEMENT ESSENTIAL?

Performance management supports overall business goals by linking the work of each individual employee and manager to the overall mission of his or her work unit. All employees, therefore, play a key role in the success of their company or organization. How well you manage the performance of your employees directly affects not only the performance of the individual employee and your work unit but also the performance of the entire company.

When employees are clear about what is expected of them and have the necessary support to contribute to an organization efficiently and productively, their sense of purpose, self-worth, and motivation will increase.

Exercise 1.2

1. Think of a time in your professional life when you were **unclear** about what was expected of you and how your job related to the overall goals of the organization. Describe your personal behavior and your performance results.

_____

_____

_____

2. Think of a time in your professional life when you were **clear** about what was expected of you and how your job related to the overall goals of the organization. Describe your personal behavior and your performance results.

_____

_____

_____

You probably discovered a large difference between your responses to the two items in Exercise 1.2. Generally, you will find a direct correlation between goal and objective clarity *and* productivity. The clearer people are about what is expected of them and how their individual efforts contribute to the whole, the more focused and rewarding their efforts become. Even if you are a self-starter, you can lose time trying to figure out what you should be doing. Taking wrong guesses can be costly.

HOW DOES PERFORMANCE MANAGEMENT WORK?

You manage performance by letting employees know:

- What is expected of them.
- How they are doing based on those expectations.
- How they may improve on the job.
- When they are doing a good job.

Performance management generally involves you and your employees in three stages of a complete review cycle. They include:

1. Performance and development planning.
2. Interim coaching and progress reviews.
3. Performance appraisal and development review.

Figure 1.2 illustrates this cycle. How carefully you carry out each of these stages makes a difference to your employees and to the accomplishment of your business objectives. You have an impact on each of these stages.

FIGURE 1.2   THE PERFORMANCE MANAGEMENT CYCLE

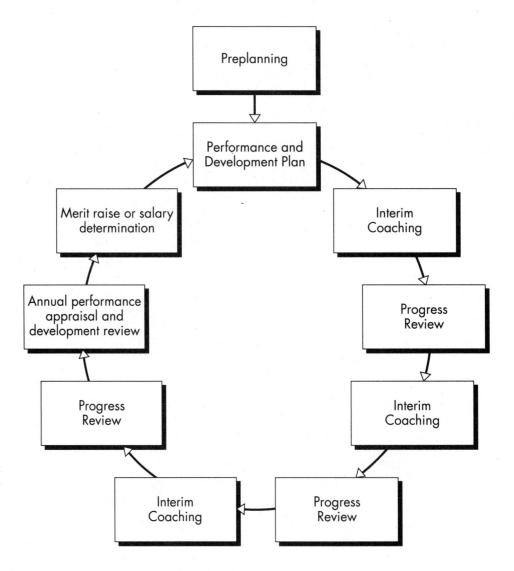

Chapter Checkpoints

✓ Performance management links an organization's overall business goals to the work of every employee or manager.

✓ Organization goals can be accomplished only through the efforts of individual employees.

✓ Employees need clear goals and ongoing feedback for continuous improvement.

✓ Performance management involves three key stages:

- Performance and development planning.
- Interim coaching and progress reviews.
- Performance appraisal and development review.

2 | Establishing Clear Goals and Objectives

This chapter will help you to:

- Define goals and objectives.
- Identify the elements of effective objectives.
- Write objectives.
- Distinguish objectives from activities.

Sarah Kramer has been a sales representative at Peabody Productions for the past six months, reporting to Vincent Valdez, a seasoned sales manager. Vincent recently learned about the company's new effort to institute an effective performance management system. In an attempt to do his job well, Vincent developed annual performance objectives for Sarah, which he gave to her. They read as follows:

1. To achieve excellent customer relations.
2. To increase sales.
3. To write reports.
4. To read sales materials tomorrow.
5. To develop yourself.

Sitting perplexed in her office, Sarah read the objectives over and over again, unable to make any sense of them. Later, thinking she did not understand Vincent's objectives because she was relatively new to the company, Sarah showed them to one of her co-workers, Mark Goldstein. Unfortunately, Mark laughed and said, "Oh, don't worry; that's just his style. He's famous for this. You'll get the hang of working with him sooner or later." ■

◼ Questions to Consider

1. What do you think is wrong with Vincent's performance objectives?

_____

_____

_____

2. Based on the fact that these are annual objectives, do you see any objectives that do not belong on Vincent's list, even if they were well written?

_____

_____

_____

3. What should Sarah do to develop her performance, based on the objectives given to her?

_____

_____

_____

2

4. How do you think these objectives might affect Sarah's behavior and performance?

_____

_____

_____

5. If you were Sarah's supervisor, how would you revise her objectives? Write your revisions below.

a. _____

b. _____

c. _____

d. _____

e. _____

Suggested solutions appear at the end of this chapter.

SETTING GOALS

The first step in the performance and development planning stage is to establish individual performance goals and objectives that directly correlate with the overall goals of the organization. Although goals and objectives were defined in Chapter 1, take a closer look here.

Goals are statements of general direction or intent. They describe conditions that will exist on a continuing basis when the manager, department, or other division is fulfilling its mission. They are broad, timeless, and unconcerned with particular achievement within a specific time period. **Goals are aspirations.**

Objectives are specific statements that describe results to be achieved, when, and by whom, in order for a goal to be accomplished. They are quantifiable and/or observable achievements that can be measured. They should be clearly differentiated from activities or strategies employed to attain them. **Objectives are expectations.**

Every objective must relate to a goal as well as to the overall mission of the organization. This cascading, or waterfall, effect was graphically depicted in Figure 1.1 on page 4.

■ **Exercise 2.1**

Respond by indicating "true" or "false" to each of the following statements.

_____   1. Goals are general statements.

_____   2. Goals have no time limits.

_____   3. Objectives may be stated in general terms.

_____   4. Objectives are time-bound.

_____   5. Objectives do not show observable achievements.

_____   6. Objectives should be very specific.

_____   7. It is not necessary for objectives to be linked to established goals of the organization.

_____   8. Objectives tell the strategies or activities employed to reach the desired result.

_____   9. Objectives describe results to be achieved.

_____   10. Goals describe results to be achieved.

_____   11. Objectives should relate to goals.

_____   12. Goals should relate to the overall mission of an organization.

■ **Exercise 2.2**

Identify the following statements by writing _G_ before each goal and _O_ before each objective.

_____   1. To improve the quality of customer service.

_____   2. By January of this year, 90 percent or more of the management staff will demonstrate understanding of the selection interviewing and performance management system to be used at Company X.

_____   3. To reduce wasted paper in the Print Shop by 5 percent over the next three months.

_____   4. To promote more cooperative attitudes among company employees.

_____   5. To reduce the monthly average of products rejected by 10% over the previous year during the next 12 months.

_____   6. To process customer order forms faster.

_____   7. To reduce waste and loss in the company.

Check your answers to Exercises 2.1 and 2.2 in the Solutions at the end of this book. If your answers are correct, move on to the next section. If you made many errors, you may want to review before moving on.

EFFECTIVE OBJECTIVES

Objectives should include:

1. The performer(s) (who)
2. The action or performance (what)
3. A time element (when)
4. An evaluation method (how you know results were achieved)
5. The place (where appropriate)

In well-stated objectives, actions or performances should be described with action verbs. These action verbs should be as *specific* and *measurable* as possible. **"To reduce," "to increase,"** and **"to demonstrate"** are more effective action verbs than **"to control," "to organize," "to understand," "to have knowledge of,"** or **"to appreciate."**

Objectives should be written in specific terms to make results clear and observable to other people. It is much more specific to state **"to increase revenue from 30 percent to 40 percent"** than it is to state **"to show an understanding of the need to increase revenue."** Specific dates or time periods for accomplishments are also very useful when writing objectives—**"to produce 100 widgets by January 1, 19___"** or **"to produce 100 widgets over the next 30 days,"** for example.

End results described in well-stated objectives should be realistic and attainable with "stretch." Employees will be required to stretch beyond their current performance or productivity.

One way to check that your objectives are well written is to use the acronym **SMART**. Ask yourself if your objectives are **s**pecific, **m**easurable, **a**ttainable, **r**esults-oriented, and **t**ime-bound.

Specific: Work objectives must be clear, concise, and simple to understand. Someone not familiar with your work area should be able to read the objective quickly and easily and understand the nature of the work.

2

*M*easurable: Objectives must be measurable and quantifiable wherever possible. Examination of completed work should lead to a determination of whether objectives were accomplished. Manager and employee need to agree on a way to measure this.

*A*ttainable: Although objectives should stretch and challenge an employee's capabilities, they must be within reach.

*R*esults-oriented: Objectives should focus on results to be achieved.

*T*ime-bound: Objectives should be time-bound and trackable. Manager and employee should be able to monitor progress toward the objective in order to allow mid-course corrections.

Exercise 2.3

Fill in the blanks.

1. Action verbs used to describe objectives should be (s) _____ and (m) _____.

2. A good way to check an objective is to use the acronym _____, which stands for _____, _____, _____, _____, and _____.

Answer the following question.

3. Why is the term *stretch* used when describing criteria for objectives?

   _____

   _____

   _____

Read the objective below; then answer the questions that follow.

To reduce the monthly backlog of orders processed by Department X from 30 percent to 15 percent by December 31 of this year.

4. *Who* is the performer? _____

5. *What* will be accomplished? (action or performance expected)

   _____

6. *What* is the time element? (when) _____

7. How will *evaluation* be determined? _____

_____

Check your answers to Exercise 2.3 in the Solutions at the end of this book. Continue on to the next section if your answers are correct. Stop and review if you made errors.

HOW TO WRITE OBJECTIVES

As a manager, your key responsibility is to produce results. You can accomplish this through leadership and use of resources. One way to view your job is to use a "systems" approach. As shown in Figure 2.1, you begin by taking *inputs* (assets and resources) and applying them in such a way (*activities*) that you produce *outputs* greater than the original inputs. In other words, you **add value** by utilizing resources.

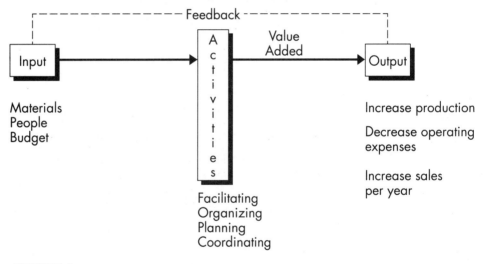

FIGURE 2.1

Objectives are statements based on outputs or end results. Objectives should *not* be activities. **Always write objectives in terms of end results, not in terms of activities.**

Exercise 2.4

Complete the following items as they apply to your present job situation.

1. List some of your inputs (tangible and intangible).

_____

_____

_____

_____

2. List some of your activities (things you do; things you spend time and effort on).

_____

_____

_____

_____

3. List your outputs (results; the value you have added).

_____

_____

_____

_____

4. In which of the three areas listed above would you want to develop goals and objectives?

_____

_____

_____

_____

Your answers to Exercise 2.4 may include a variety of examples.

Inputs:	**Activities:**	**Outputs:**
People	Planning	Quality customer service
Time	Organizing	Revenue earned
Money	Coordinating	Revenue saved
Equipment	Directing	Sales made
Supplies	Developing	Products made
	Supporting	Products developed
	Training	

Develop goals and objectives to lead to outputs. Objectives are not written for inputs or activities. Don't concern yourself with finding the best way to reach output until you have identified the desired output itself.

OBJECTIVES VERSUS ACTIVITIES

Now you know the difference between goals and objectives and the importance of being *specific* when writing objectives. An additional problem with writing objectives is the *activity trap*. Remember, objectives are statements of results to be achieved. They do *not* tell what activities are needed to implement the objectives.

Many times managers look at a problem area, then focus on *activities* to help alleviate the problem. When studying a problem area that needs to be corrected, the manager should ask himself or herself, "What do I want to have happen as a result?" The answer to this question should **not** be a list of activities that may not produce the desired end result. Avoid the activity trap.

■ Exercise 2.5

Situation 1: A sales manager has been charged with a difficult task. She needs to increase overall sales during the next 12 months by 10 percent over last year. She plans to ask her sales representatives to work hand-in-hand with the research and development and the marketing departments to accomplish this task. The manager needs help in writing her objectives. Write one for her.

_____

_____

_____

_____

_____

_____

_____

_____

_____

_____

2

Situation 2: A customer service manager is concerned about the number of complaints and product returns. As a special project for this fiscal year, he would like to aim for a 10 percent reduction in customer complaints. He plans to prepare and deliver a customer relations program for his staff, then monitor its progress. Write an objective that would allow the manager and his department to know whether or not they have accomplished this special project.

_____

_____

_____

_____

_____

_____

_____

_____

_____

_____

The objectives you wrote in Exercise 2.5 should be similar to the following:

Situation 1: The sales department will increase product sales by 10 percent over last year over the next 12 months. (Specific dates can be substituted for the next 12 months.) Your objective is incorrect if you included any statements concerning training, sales incentives, or forms of collaboration involving the research and development or marketing departments. Such statements are activities, not desired end results. Don't fall into the activity trap.

Situation 2: The customer service department will reduce the number of customer complaints regarding product returns by 10 percent over last year during the next 12 months. (Specific dates can be substituted for the next 12 months.) Your objective is incorrect if you included plans to prepare and deliver a customer relations program for the staff. A customer relations program will not necessarily resolve customer complaints or stop product returns.

Exercise 2.6

1. In your own words, define the following terms.

Goal: _____

_____

Objective: _____

_____

2. Objectives should include the following elements:

a. _____

b. _____

c. _____

d. _____

e. _____

2

3. Circle the correct response. Objectives should be developed in the area of:

a. Inputs

b. Activities

c. Outputs

4. When writing performance objectives, be sure to avoid the _____

_____.

5. Using SMART as your criteria, rewrite the following goal as an objective:

To increase support for the United Way.

_____

6. Write an example of an objective that you would submit to your supervisor. Be sure it complies with the criteria described in this chapter.

_____

_____

_____

Check your answers in the Solutions at the end of this book.*

Chapter Appendix: Solutions to page 12.

1. Vincent's performance objectives were far too vague.

2. Objective 4 did not belong on Vincent's annual objectives list because it was a short-term objective.

3. Objective 5 was the only objective that related to Sarah's development at all. And it was far too vague to provide Sarah with any direction.

_____

*Solutions to Exercises 2.1, 2.2, 2.3, and 2.6 are located on pages 121-122.

4. Sarah, no doubt, could become frustrated and confused. She might waste energy and effort guessing what she should do. In the process, she would be unproductive.

5. Check your objectives to see if they are SMART. The following is an example of how Vincent's objectives could have been revised:
   a. To reduce the average number of customer complaints received by 10 percent over the next fiscal year.
   b. To increase this year's (date) sales by 20 percent over the last fiscal year.
   c. To write and submit monthly sales reports based upon company specifications.
   d. To attend and successfully complete the company sales training program during the first six months of employment (date).
   e. (Answers will vary greatly.)

Chapter Checkpoints

✓ Goals are broad, general statements, timeless and unconcerned with specific achievement.

✓ Objectives are measurable and specific statements of results to be achieved.

✓ Effective objectives include the following elements: who, what, where, when, and how.

✓ Use the acronym **SMART** (**s**pecific, **m**easurable, **a**ttainable, **r**esults-oriented, and **t**ime-bound) to test how well you have written your objectives.

✓ Avoid the activity trap when writing objectives. Objectives are desired end results, **not** the activities or strategies necessary to achieve them.

3 | Performance and Development Planning

This chapter will help you to:

- Recognize the importance of performance planning.
- Define performance and development planning.
- Understand how and when performance and development planning should be done.

The chief executive officer (CEO) for P. M. Manufacturing Company has just issued a memo to all managers asking for a mid-year status report on meeting the company's annual goals. This year, emphasis has been placed on developing new accounts. Norman Chan, the director of sales, decides to individually meet with all the employees who report directly to him so that each can give him information to respond to the CEO's request.

The first employee is Terence Nystrom, a junior account manager. Norman opens the conversation by asking, "How are you doing on those company goals?"

Terence looks puzzled and says, "What company goals?"

Norman replies, "You know, the ones the company gave me about six months ago."

Terence squirms in his chair with growing uneasiness and says, hesitantly, "I don't think you ever told me about those."

Frazzled, Norman says, "Well, never mind, then, just tell me what you've been doing for the past six months."

Terence says, "Well, I've been spending most of my time trying to reconnect with our old customer accounts to see if we could make some additional sales. It hasn't been working very well, though."

Norman sinks in his chair and then rises up in anger, shouting, "But you knew our focus this year was to increase sales by developing new accounts. Why didn't you spend your time on that?"

Terence begins to feel enraged when he thinks of all the time and energy he put into the old accounts, and he says, "Well, you never told me, so how was I supposed to know that? I did what I thought you would want me to do. You seemed to think this was fine last year."

Feelings continue to escalate between Norman and Terence. The meeting is ended abruptly by a knock on the door from Norman's next employee "victim." ■

■ Questions to Consider

1. Do you think Terence knew the company's goals?

_____

2. Do you think Terence knew what performance was expected of him and how it would be measured?

_____

3. How did Terence's knowledge, or lack of it, affect his performance and relationship with his boss?

_____

_____

4. If you were to replay this situation, what might you have done differently?

_____

_____

WHY IS PERFORMANCE AND DEVELOPMENT PLANNING IMPORTANT?

The overall purpose of performance and development planning is to

1. Make performance expectations explicit.
2. Tie individual performance to organization and department business plans.
3. Identify measurement or evaluation criteria for performance.
4. Identify "gaps" in knowledge or skills required to achieve expectations.
5. Describe specific development activities.
6. Foster communication between manager and employee.

> Items 1, 2, and 3 are considered aspects of performance planning, and items 4 and 5 are considered aspects of development planning. Item 6, fostering communication between manager and employee, is essential to all stages of performance management.

WHAT IS PERFORMANCE AND DEVELOPMENT PLANNING?

Planning starts off the performance management cycle. Here you must review your business plans and decide what work needs to get done and how each of your employees fits into your plans. You and each of your employees not only need to plan work and performance expectations; you also need to choose development activities to enhance the employee's present job skills. It is important to plan for both performance and development, as planning for both creates a strong foundation for the entire performance management process.

Performance and development planning consists of:

- Developing SMART *performance* objectives with and for each employee.
- Developing SMART *development* objectives with and for each employee.
- Agreeing on a performance plan so that expectations are clear to all involved.

Performance Planning

Performance planning gives you the opportunity to discuss the following issues with each employee:

- Your expectations for his or her performance.
- How the employee's specific performance objectives tie into your department's business plans and the organization's goals.

Performance plans generally focus on five to six year-long objectives that reflect the key areas of employee responsibility. Once these have been discussed and agreed on, you should write the performance objectives into a formal performance plan. If your organization has a standard form for this, use it; otherwise, refer to the sample Performance and Development Plan shown in Figure 3.1. The first section of this form covers performance objectives, and the second covers development objectives, which we will discuss later in this chapter.

Creating Performance Objectives

Performance objectives provide the basis for your interim coaching, progress reviews, and year-end review. Here are some sample performance objectives:

1. (Sales) To develop five new key accounts that represent gross sales of over $10,000 each by December 31 of this year.

2. (Customer service) To respond to all customer questions and/or complaints for ABC Department within 24 hours of their receipt.

3. (Manufacturing) To increase on-time delivery by 20 percent over the prior year, during the next 12 months, December to January 19___.

4. (Marketing) To produce all monthly company newsletters for printing by the 15th of each month and ensure distribution to all employees by the 25th of each month.

5. (Administrative/clerical) To type, proofread, and adjust for accuracy all required reports for X unit within three days of their receipt throughout the year.

◼ Exercise 3.1

Try out your skills in writing performance objectives by writing down two performance objectives for one direct report. They should capture a significant area of a person's job responsibilities so they could later be used as criteria to evaluate part of the person's overall job performance. Use the SMART criteria.

Performance objectives:

1. _____
   _____
   _____

2. _____
   _____
   _____

FIGURE 3.1
**SAMPLE WORKSHEET FOR CREATING PERFORMANCE AND
DEVELOPMENT OBJECTIVES**

Key: Weighting (0-100%) based on importance of objective to overall job accomplishment

Operational/Business Objectives:

1. Performance objective	Measurement criteria
Weight (% of total job)	
2. Performance objective	Measurement criteria
Weight (% of total job)	
3. Performance objective	Measurement criteria
Weight (% of total job)	
4. Performance objective	Measurement criteria
Weight (% of total job)	
5. Performance objective	Measurement criteria
Weight (% of total job)	
6. Performance objective	Measurement criteria
Weight (% of total job)	

Development Objectives:

1. Development objective	Action plan
2. Development objective	Action plan
3. Development objective	Action plan

Signature and Dates:

Employee name:_____ Job title:_____

Office or department/division: _____

Measurement period: __/__/__ to __/__/__   Date prepared:_____

Signature of employee:_____ Signature of manager:_____

                    Date:_____   Date:_____

Additional signatures per company policy: Name: _____ Position:_____

                                        Name: _____ Position:_____

Development Planning

Development planning provides a means of helping an employee maintain or enhance the knowledge, skills, and abilities needed to do his or her current job. As jobs change, it is your responsibility to help the employee identify and obtain new skills and knowledge.

Employee development often focuses on:

- On-the-job training.
- Special projects, assignments.
- Cross-training or rotations to other jobs.
- Self-study.
- Training (internal and external courses).
- Mentoring.
- Attendance at conferences, seminars, and workshops.
- Reading material.
- Membership in professional organizations or associations.

Creating Development Objectives

Consider your department's priorities and workload, the specific knowledge and skills that need developing, and your particular employee in deciding on the right development objectives. After you discuss performance plans with the employee, you will want to discuss these development plans. The second section of Figure 3.1 provides a place for you to list development objectives.

Planning must be done to make expectations explicit and to prevent surprises. An employee should never be surprised by his or her appraisal at the end of the measurement period. Involving the employee in performance planning at the start of a performance cycle and maintaining dialogue ensures that your employee will be keyed into your expectations.

Development Objectives

1. (General Management) To complete successfully our six-month company training program for managers by July 1, 19____.

2. (Human Resources) To attend at least eight monthly professional meetings per year sponsored by X (specify name of organization) human resources organization.

3. (General) To cross-train for and serve a week's rotation on at least one new job within the division (e.g., Job A, B, C, or D) every six months.

4. (General) To learn how to use X software on the personal computer by the end of the first quarter and then to use it throughout the year as needed for job tasks.

■ Exercise 3.2

Practice your development planning skills by writing two development objectives. Think of an employee who reports to you. If you are not currently supervising someone, write development objectives for yourself. As you write your objectives, be sure to consider:

- Knowledge and/or skills to be developed or strengthened. These should be based on a current analysis of job needs as well as individual needs and interests.
- Development activities and target dates. These may include, for example, work assignments as well as additional training such as on-the-job courses, seminars, and college programs.

Development objectives:

1. _____
   _____
   _____

2. _____
   _____
   _____

WHEN SHOULD YOU DO PERFORMANCE AND DEVELOPMENT PLANNING?

There are many times when you will need to be involved in performance and development planning activities. For the most part, planning should be conducted:

- Annually, at the start of each performance and development review cycle.

Other key times include:

- When a new employee is hired and you want to establish clear performance goals and objectives.
- When an employee is transferred to your department and needs expectations to be clarified.
- After companywide, division, or department business plans are completed or revised.

3

Chapter Checkpoints

✓ Performance and development plans enable a manager to tie individual efforts to overall organizational goals and to define performance expectations and standards clearly.

✓ Performance and development planning should be done when:

- Hiring or transfering employees.

- Business plans are newly developed.

- Annual performance and development reviews have been completed.

4 | Planning Meetings

This chapter will help you to:

- Identify specific responsibilities for everyone involved in performance and development planning.
- Prepare and conduct performance and development planning meetings.
- Follow up on performance and development planning meetings.

Maria Alvarez, a claims manager for Family Mutual Insurance Company, has planned a performance and development planning meeting with her employee Curtis Littlejohn. Curtis has been with Family Mutual for the past seven years and, like many employees there, was promoted from within. He has held his current position as claims supervisor for two years and has been doing well. Everyone who works with Curtis admires him for his perseverance and ability to learn quickly.

Curtis entered Maria's office for the meeting, looking forward to discussing his goals and objectives for the coming year. With hardly a greeting, Maria dived into the meeting, spending the first 30 minutes spouting off 15 new performance objectives and standards for Curtis to achieve over the next fiscal year. The new objectives were above and beyond Curtis's existing goals and responsibilities.

During the meeting, no priorities for the new objectives were given, and Maria never stopped to ask Curtis for his input, agreement, or commitment to the new objectives. All the objectives involved a major time commitment from Curtis, and he already was carrying a caseload of some 300 claims.

Curtis, being naturally quiet, sat in silence, thinking how unrealistic and unfair the objectives were. His workload was already unbearable, and he had been working a lot of overtime hours just to keep up. Now Maria had handed him 15 more difficult tasks. Curtis does not know how he will ever accomplish them. ■

■ Questions to Consider

1. What do you think went wrong in the meeting?

_____

_____

2. What do you think Curtis will do as a result of the meeting?

_____

_____

3. How could this affect his performance?

_____

_____

4. If you were Curtis's manager, what might you have done differently during this meeting?

_____

_____

It is 4:30 P.M. Eartha Washington, a software development manager, stops Fred Weissman, one of her software engineers, in the hallway. Eartha says, ''Oh, I forgot to tell you, we need to meet on those performance and development plans today! They're due tomorrow. Can you be in my office in five minutes?'' Fred, who has been on the job for only three months, looks a bit dazed, having no idea what performance and development plans are. So as not to rock the boat with his new manager, he says, ''Yes,'' and shows up in Eartha's office five minutes later.

Eartha spends the first few minutes of the meeting scrambling through reams of unorganized paperwork. ''Oh, here it is,'' she says, as she takes out a blank performance and development plan with directions sent from Human Resources in a memo dated two months ago.

''It says here that I'm supposed to let you know what your performance goals are this year. Well, why don't you write some down and give them to me by morning. As long as they seem okay, I'll approve them.''

4

Fred again says, "Okay," but inside he is feeling quite frustrated. He does not have a clue about how to get started. He has been at the company for only a short while, and Eartha has never told him what she expects of him, much less what the company expects.

Fred is beginning to wonder what he is getting into with this new job. ■

■ Questions to Consider

1. What do you think went wrong?

_____

_____

2. What do you think Fred will do as a result of this meeting?

_____

_____

3. How could this affect his performance?

_____

_____

4. What would you have done differently if you were Fred's manager?

_____

_____

MANAGER AND EMPLOYEE RESPONSIBILITIES

Many of us have probably felt like Curtis Littlejohn or Fred Weissman at one time or another. To avoid Maria Alvarez's and Eartha Washington's mistakes, you need to know how to make your performance and development planning meetings effective. These meetings are extremely important; they affect not only performance but also your ongoing relationships with employees. You will need to prepare for them adequately, conduct them well, and follow up on them.

After you have developed some initial performance and development plans for your employees, you must communicate them in a performance and development meeting. It is key that these are realistic plans reflecting job priorities. At this stage, each employee learns what is expected of him or her and clarifies his or her work responsibilities. Equally important, both you and your employee must agree on goals and objectives and must be committed to carrying them out.

The Manager's Responsibilities

- Develop general objectives for each employee based on the organization's goals, the department's business plan, and the manager's performance plan.
- Schedule a performance and development planning discussion with each employee.
- Assist all employees in determining priorities and/or identifying critical objectives for their areas of responsibility.
- Review each subordinate's draft performance plan:
  a. Check for technical completeness of objectives, performance standards, and target dates for completion. Are they SMART?
  b. Determine whether there is sufficient authority to carry out the objectives and whether needed resources can be provided.
- Assist employees in determining development areas and activities.
- Maintain an up-to-date file on each employee's objectives.
- Develop monitoring methods to use with employees to ensure continuous progress.
- *If the business plan changes significantly*, work with each employee to alter the employee's objectives to reflect these changes.

The Employee's Responsibilities

- Familiarize yourself with organization and department goals and objectives, wherever possible.
- Develop preliminary objectives that are SMART, with clear performance standards and completion deadlines.
- Prepare supporting data for each objective.
- Decide what resources and coordination will be needed.
- List questions and potential problems for discussion with manager.
- Assess current skill level requirements to meet the performance plan objectives, and consider what skills or abilities need to be developed.

- Develop preliminary development activities to assist in accomplishing objectives.
- Discuss draft plan with manager.
- Renegotiate objectives with manager if major changes occur.

PREPARING FOR THE MEETING

The Preplanning Meeting

To make performance and development planning work, a *preplanning meeting* with your employee is strongly recommended. To prepare for the preplanning meeting:

- Review the business objectives for your unit or department.
- Inform the employee about the meeting, its purpose, and the agenda at least one week in advance.
- Schedule enough uninterrupted time.
- Select a place that is private and comfortable.
- Ask the employee to prepare a draft list of performance objectives and development activities.
- Prepare a preliminary plan for the employee, including specific performance objectives, measurement criteria with target dates, and development objectives with action plans. Use an updated job description, the employee's prior performance plan (if available), and your department's business plan to help you.
- Finally, ask yourself the following questions:
  What is the current skill level of the employee?
  What skill level can I reasonably expect the employee to attain?
  How will I measure the performance of each objective during the review period?
  How many performance objectives are reasonable relative to the person and the job?
  What supports and resources are necessary to assist the employee in fulfilling the requirements of the performance plan?
  Are the necessary supports and resources available?
  Are completion dates required for the objective(s)? If so, what are those dates?

■ **E x e r c i s e   4 . 1**

Plan a performance and development "preplanning" meeting for one of your employees. Use the material you already have developed in previous chapters. A good starting point would be to refer to the performance and development objectives you listed in Chapter 3.

CONDUCTING THE MEETING

Follow these steps when conducting the meeting:

4

1. *Briefly reiterate the main purpose of the discussion.*

2. *Review and discuss the ideas you developed for the* **performance** *plan.*
   a. Specific performance objectives linked to the business plan.
   b. Indicators of how well the objectives are met (measurement standards).
   c. Target dates.

3. *Review the employee's input and consider ways to incorporate it into the plan.*

4. *Be sure your performance plan is clear.* Carefully review everything on the performance plan. Make sure all expectations and related issues are absolutely clear. Listen to what the employee has to say and ask the employee to paraphase:
   a. The specifics of the plan.
   b. What commitment is expected on the employee's part.

5. *Review, discuss, and complete the* **development** *plan.* Be sure it contains specific development activities tied to your business plan, supports, and resources available to the employee, and can be put into action.

6. *Be sure everything in the development plan is* clear and that your employee understands and agrees with the commitment you expect.

7. *Employee and manager sign, date, and keep a copy of the plan* for monitoring, coaching, and review purposes.

■ **E x e r c i s e   4 . 2**

Now that you've prepared for a meeting, role-play a meeting with a colleague acting as your employee. Next, switch roles. Use Figure 4.1 on page 42 as a guideline for your meetings.

4

MEETING FOLLOW-UP

To follow up on a meeting:

- Review the completed performance and development plan with your manager. If changes are needed, inform the employee, discuss the changes as necessary, and modify the plans.
- During the review cycle, periodically review plans to be sure that they are still current and in line with company goals and objectives. Whenever there is a major change in priorities or projects, consider how the plans will be affected. Make whatever changes are necessary, and be sure to discuss them with your employee.

FIGURE 4.1

Performance and Development Planning Meeting Feedback Form

1. Were the performance objectives stated clearly and specifically?   YES   NO

2. Were the performance objectives:
Specific?   YES   NO
Measurable?   YES   NO
Attainable?   YES   NO
Results-oriented?   YES   NO
Time-bound?   YES   NO

3. Were priorities set, if applicable?   YES   NO

4. Were obstacles for reaching these objectives discussed?   YES   NO

5. Were performance standards or measurements clearly explained?   YES   NO

6. Were performance objectives and standards agreed on?   YES   NO

Chapter Checkpoints

✓ Managers are responsible for developing, maintaining, updating, and monitoring performance and development plans for each of their employees. Subordinates should have input into performance and development plans.

✓ Managers and employees need to prepare for performance and development planning meetings.

✓ Meetings should be conducted to allow two-way dialogue between manager and employee.

✓ Follow-up to performance planning meetings include:

- Communicating plans to your manager according to company practice and policy.

- Adjusting plans as necessary based upon employee input or changes in business plans.

5 | Interim Coaching

This chapter will help you to:

- Define interim coaching.
- Recognize when and why you should provide interim coaching.
- Learn guidelines for giving useful feedback.

Ed Boroski has been an accountant for American Healthcare Providers, Inc., for 11 months. When he first came to his job, his manager, Linda Menrad, discussed initial performance and development plans for the year. During that year, the billing department (to which he was assigned) experienced a great deal of turnover in the professional and clerical staff. Ed found himself having to give up many of his initial performance and development plans in order to pitch in to keep the department going. He spent most of his time in areas outside his original scope of responsibility. His boss was an experienced crisis manager, continually assigning him new tasks at the last minute, without any regard for previously assigned work.

One morning, Linda called Ed into her office to discuss his performance. She started by saying, "I'm sorry we haven't been able to sit down earlier this year, but, as you know, our department has been experiencing a lot of changes. You may recall that, at the start of your employment, we established some annual performance and development goals. I need to tell you that your annual review is coming up in a month, and based on the plans we agreed upon, I'm very disappointed in you. It appears you haven't even tried to make any progress on these goals, and

because of this, the whole department will end up falling short of company expectations. I suggest you review these goals again and see if you can fix this over the next 30 days. If you do not catch up, I'll be forced to recommend probationary status. We just can't let this kind of performance continue!'' ■

Questions to Consider

1. If you were Ed, how would you respond to this situation?

_____

_____

2. What do you feel Linda did wrong?

_____

_____

3. What impact do you think Linda's actions might have on Ed's performance?

_____

_____

4. Is there anything Ed could have done differently to manage this situation before it reached this point?

_____

_____

5. If you were Ed's manager, how might you have managed the situation differently?

_____

_____

WHAT IS INTERIM COACHING?

Rather than wait until the annual appraisal review, it is imperative that managers provide ongoing performance feedback, or _interim coaching_. This feedback should be based on agreed-on performance plans that have been continually updated to reflect shifts in company goals or department needs.

Regular feedback, positive _and_ negative, is critical to a successful performance management system. The degree of formality and length of feedback depends on the situation. In some cases, a planned discussion is in order; at other times a few informal words may do the trick.

■ Exercise 5.1

Consider the last full year of your employment and answer the following questions.

1. Were you evaluated on established and agreed-on performance goals, which had been updated as needed?

_____

2. How often did coaching or feedback occur throughout the year?

_____

Coaching is most effective when it is based on agreed-on goals that have been updated as needed. Effective ongoing coaching should occur at least quarterly.

WHEN TO PROVIDE INTERIM COACHING?

When Strengths and Accomplishments Are Recognized.   Employees need to know that you recognize and appreciate what they are doing well. If performance has been high, if there are notable accomplishments, and if you recognize strengths, commend the employee in an appropriate way.

When Performance Needs Improvement.   If performance is slipping for any reason, or targets have been missed, you need to speak with the employee immediately and coach for improvement. An employee can then take corrective action and still be successful in achieving his or her goals.

When Growth and Development Are Necessary.   At times, employees must grow and develop to meet the current and future demands of their jobs. Discussions of this nature should be held as needed.

When Projects and/or Priorities Change.   Change is healthy for companies, but needs to be acknowledged as it affects individual performance goals throughout the review period. If there are changes in projects and/or priorities that affect the performance and development plan, they need to be communicated as they happen. Both you and your employee share joint responsibility for ensuring that performance and development plans are updated and that new objectives or development activities are set up to meet these changes.

Performance feedback discussions should be ongoing and should take place whenever necessary. Most often, they consist of brief and informal discussions.

Regardless of how often you have informal discussions with your employees, feedback must be formalized at times. It is recommended that at least one formal coaching discussion, the *progress review*, should be scheduled and conducted every 90 days. (Chapter 9 covers progress reviews in depth.)

Exercise 5.2

Think again about the last year of your employment. Describe briefly your experiences with the following types of coaching:

1. When strengths and accomplishments were recognized: _____
   _____
   _____

2. When performance needed improvement: _____
   _____
   _____

3. When growth and development were necessary: _____
   _____
   _____

4. When projects and/or priorities changed: _____
   _____
   _____

5

Balanced coaching is essential. Far too often employees hear what they are doing **wrong**, not what they are doing **right**. As a result, employees tend to become demotivated. Quite often, changes in projects or priorities are not clearly communicated and agreed on up-front. This often causes employees to feel overwhelmed, never really knowing whether they are on the right track. As in the opening case study, changes can cause unnecessary surprises during progress reviews or annual reviews.

WHY PROVIDE INTERIM COACHING?

Interim coaching is used to provide feedback on performance and to review and update goals. Keep in mind that:

- Feedback keeps good performance on track by recognizing and reinforcing positive behaviors.
- Feedback enables employees to improve their performance by letting them know how to redirect or change certain behaviors to achieve success.
- Feedback enables employees to grow and develop.
- In reviewing and updating goals, feedback enables employees to adjust their work efforts and shift their focus as company priorities and goals change.

■ Exercise 5.3

Consider your responses to the questions in Exercises 5.1 and 5.2. Summarize the impact of the coaching you received by answering the questions below.

1. How did the coaching feel? _____
   _____

2. How did the coaching affect your performance? _____
   _____

Well-executed coaching usually is a positive experience and helps a person feel supported in his or her efforts. Effective and ongoing coaching generally affects performance favorably.

GUIDELINES FOR USEFUL PERFORMANCE FEEDBACK

Feedback is the primary means for recognizing good performance and for redirecting behavior that needs to be improved. Feedback helps individuals to keep their behavior on target and achieve their goals. Whether you are giving positive or negative feedback, it is important to keep the following guidelines in mind.

1. *Feedback should be descriptive rather than evaluative.* Descriptive language leaves the individual free to use the feedback as he or she sees fit. Avoiding evaluative language averts possible defensiveness.
2. *Feedback should be specific rather than general.* Whether positive or negative, specific feedback is much more meaningful than general feedback. To be told that you are "dominating" is not as useful as to be told, "Just now when we were discussing solutions to the problem, you did not allow others equal time to share their suggestions, and you interrupted when you heard ideas you did not agree with."
3. *Feedback should be directed toward behavior that can be addressed.* Frustration is increased when a person is reminded of some shortcoming over which he or she has no control.
4. *Feedback should be well-timed.* In general, feedback is most useful at the earliest opportunity after a particular behavior has occurred.
5. *Feedback should be checked to ensure clear communication.* Have the receiver rephrase the feedback and confirm that it corresponds to your intent.

6. *Feedback should be "owned" by the giver. Use personal pronouns such as "I" and "my."* "I messages" enable the giver to take responsibility for his or her thoughts, feelings, and reactions.

7. *Feedback should be based on observed behavior.* Inferences or assumptions should not be used to support feedback. Observe the employee's behavior before giving feedback. Gather information from the employee using open-ended questions to ensure that you have all relevant and necessary information before drawing conclusions.

8. *Feedback should be balanced.* Maintain a supportive, positive climate. Limit negative feedback to comments on one or two items at a time. An employee cannot improve everything at once.

▮ Exercise 5.4

Using the guidelines for useful performance feedback, rewrite the following statements to make them more effective. If it helps to bring in specific situations as you rewrite the statements, do so.

1. "You're not even trying to do your job correctly."

_____

_____

2. "You're always late for work."

_____

_____

3. "I don't like your attitude."

_____

_____

4. "Last month you . . ."

_____

_____

5. "I'm sure you know what I'm talking about."

_____

_____

6. "The company is disappointed in you."

_____

_____

7. "Yesterday, one of your peers told me that you . . ."

_____

_____

8. "You never seem to be able to do anything right."

_____

_____

Sample Solution

1. "When you make an error in processing orders, it affects our customer relations negatively."
2. "Today and yesterday you were an hour late for work."
3. "When you openly criticize the company in our department meetings, it negatively affects our ability to solve problems in a positive way."
4. "A moment ago you . . ."
5. "Could you summarize your understanding of what we're talking about?"
6. "I am disappointed in your performance regarding . . ."
7. "Yesterday, I observed you . . ."
8. "I know you'll be able to resolve this problem. I think well of you and know how much you want to contribute to this department."

Exercise 5.5

Using the guidelines for useful performance feedback, develop a script for giving feedback on a specific performance objective. This feedback can be positive, negative, or both. It can be directed at one of your employees or at yourself. If you choose yourself, you may want to take the opportunity to rescript a previous feedback experience that you feel did not go well.

Feedback script: _____

_____

_____

_____

_____

_____

_____

_____

Exercise 5.6

Role-play with a partner the feedback script you generated in Exercise 5.5. Ask your partner to critique your performance by following the guidelines for useful performance feedback. After your effort has been critiqued, switch roles. Use the feedback and critique form below.

Feedback and Critique Form

1. Was the feedback descriptive rather than evaluative? _____

2. Was the feedback specific rather than general? _____

3. Was the feedback directed toward behavior that the person can do something about? _____

4. Was the feedback well-timed? _____

5. Was the feedback checked to ensure clear communication? _____

6. Was the feedback owned by the giver? _____

7. Was the feedback based on observed behavior? _____

8. Was the feedback balanced? _____

Summary comments:

Recognition of strengths and accomplishments: _____
_____
_____
_____
_____

Improvements needed: _____
_____
_____
_____
_____

Areas for growth and development: _____
_____
_____
_____
_____

5

Chapter Checkpoints

✓ Interim coaching is performance feedback based on established performance plans.

✓ Interim coaching can be formal or informal.

✓ Interim coaching should be ongoing.

✓ Interim coaching provides feedback on performance as well as opportunities to review and update performance and development plans.

✓ Feedback should be:

- Descriptive rather than evaluative.
- Specific rather than general.
- Directed toward behavior that the person can do something about.
- Well-timed.
- Checked to ensure clear communication.
- "Owned" by the giver.
- Based on observed behavior.
- Balanced.

6 | Constructive Praising

This chapter will help you to:

- Understand why some praises are more effective than others.
- Recognize when to praise people.
- Guard against common pitfalls in the praising process.
- Deliver constructive praise.

Julian Micheaux, an environmental scientist employed by the U.S. Scientific Corporation, spent three months working on an important water treatment project for the company. He felt extremely proud of his hard work and was pleased with what he had been able to accomplish in such a short time. He had gone beyond the call of duty and was hoping for acknowledgment.

Six months later, at an awards dinner, Julian learned that the company was working on a much larger international contract as a result of his initial project. At this dinner, Alexander Carmichael, Julian's supervisor, was called to the podium to accept the company's all-around achievement award for obtaining the contract. Alexander accepted the award graciously as all applauded, never once acknowledging Julian for his work on the initial project.

A month later Julian was called into Alexander's office. Finally, Julian thought, he would be getting the acknowledgment he deserved.

Alexander opened by saying, "As you know, Julian, we've won that big international contract. I thought that since you did a lot of the work on the initial project, you wouldn't mind lending a hand on this one. As it stands now, we're in the soup. There's more work here than I thought there would be, and we just don't have enough

resources to handle it. The staffers on this project aren't up to speed, so I'm sure you'll understand why I have to ask you to help us pick up the slack. The others are just too slow, and I know I can count on you to push us forward on this and not get behind in your other work." ■

Questions to Consider

1. If you were Julian, how would you respond to this situation?

_____

_____

2. What do you think went wrong?

_____

_____

3. What impact do you think this chain of events will have on Julian's performance?

_____

_____

4. If you were Julian's manager, how might you have managed the situation differently?

_____

_____

Praising is an essential ingredient to any good performance management and, therefore, it is constantly used in coaching. Far too often, employees and managers alike do not receive the praise they deserve. Many times, the value of praising people is not realized, and the knowledge of how to deliver praises effectively is lacking. This chapter will teach you the invaluable skill of constructive praising using a step-by-step approach.

THE PROCESS OF PRAISING

Praising allows you to:

- Acknowledge positive behavior.
- Keep good performance on track.
- Reinforce good performance.
- Help people feel good about themselves.
- Help people feel good about their job performances.
- Motivate people to continue doing a good job.

Why Do Some Praises Feel Better Than Others?

Generally, praises that are specific, timely, and genuine have the greatest impact on people. Vague praises can seem confusing or unsupported—they send a mixed message and even appear manipulative.

When Should You Praise People?

Learners should be praised when their performance is *approximately right*. Just as a child learns to walk step-by-step and periodically falls down, so does the new learner. Similar to the developing child, the adult learner also needs support and encouragement throughout the learning process.

Seasoned employees should be praised when they do things *exactly right*. They have developed the skills, knowledge, and confidence necessary to do their job and, therefore, should be expected to carry out their responsibilities well and with little guidance. Keep in mind that when the seasoned employee is faced with a new task, he or she becomes a learner and should be treated accordingly. Far too often, employees are set up for failure when they face new job responsibilities or challenges without guidance or support.

6

Beware

Do not say, "Yes, but . . ." Using the word *but* in any praising sentence devalues the praise, particularly if it is followed by a criticism. Always end your sentence and begin with a new one if you have other thoughts to share. This way you will not negate your own praising.

Do not assign more work when praising. Good performance should not be rewarded with assignments of more work. Many top performers experience "job dumping" and, as a result, become overwhelmed and feel set up for failure. They often become burned out and demotivated, and many leave an organization in utter frustration.

Do not "gunnysack" the recipient of praise. "Gunnysacking" is saving up undelivered communications, sometimes delivering them all at once and other times forgetting them entirely. By its very nature, gunnysacking causes your communications to lose impact because they are neither immediate nor focused. Remember, praises are most meaningful when given immediately.

HOW TO DELIVER CONSTRUCTIVE PRAISES*

1. Tell the employee what he or she did right.
   - Use specific descriptive terms when identifying the right behavior.
   - Tell the employee what the positive impact of his or her behavior is on you, the department, or the organization.

2. Tell the employee how you fell about his or her behavior.
   - Be specific.
   - Communicate how good you feel about what he or she did right.

3. Pause for a moment to allow the praising to be felt.
   - Silence allows the employee to feel your genuineness.

4. Encourage the employee to do more of the same.
   - Acknowledge and show appreciation for the right behavior.

5. Reaffirm that you value the employee and his or her performance.

---

*These suggestions for delivering constructive praise are adapted with the approval of Blanchard Training and Development Inc., from THE ONE MINUTE MANAGER by Kenneth Blanchard, Ph.D., and Spencer Johnson, M.D. Copyright 1981, 1982 by Blanchard Family Partnership and Candle Communications Corp. By permission of William Morrow & Company, Inc.

Important Tips

- Praise immediately.
- Praise approximately right behavior with learners.
- Praise exactly right behavior with experienced employees as long as they are not learning a new task.
- Focus on specific behaviors or performance, not on the individual or personality.
- Remember not to use "yes, but," not to assign more work, and not to "gunnysack."

A typical constructive praising session might sound like the one below.

1. Describe the behavior: "I noticed how quickly you helped Mrs. Jones with her water filter replacement this morning and how pleased she was by the service she received."

2. Describe how you feel about the behavior and the contribution it made to the whole: "I'm glad to see how much you care about serving our customers. That kind of personal attention is what supports our customer service goals and keeps our customers coming back."

3. Pause to allow the praise to be felt.

4. Encourage more of the same: "Thank you for taking the time you do with our customers. It really makes a difference."

5. Reaffirm the employee and his or her performance: "You're a good role model for us all. I really appreciate your efforts, and keep up the good work!"

Exercise 6.1

Think of a recent work situation where you felt a praising would have been an appropriate form of feedback. This may be a praising that you would have liked to have given to an employee, peer, boss, or even yourself. Outline your praising below.

1. Describe the behavior: _____

_____

2. Describe how you felt about the behavior and the contribution it
made to the whole:

_____

_____

3. Pause to allow the praise to be felt.

4. Encourage more of the same: _____

_____

5. Reaffirm the employee and his or her performance:

_____

_____

Once you have outlined your praising, the next step is to deliver it.
Remember, praisings are of no value if you save them up or keep them to
yourself.

Exercise 6.2

Select a partner to practice praising. Ask your partner to role-play the situation with you, taking turns in the roles of praiser and receiver. Use the
praising critique form below as a guide.

Constructive Praising Critique Form

Key: 1—Not at all; 2—Somewhat; 3—Pretty much; 4—yes.

1. Was the description of the positive behavior stated specifically and concisely?	1	2	3	4
2. Was the impact of the behavior on an individual, department, or organization stated?	1	2	3	4
3. Were the sender's feelings "owned" and shared with the receiver?	1	2	3	4
4. Did the sender pause to let what was being said sink in and allow the receiver to respond to the praising?	1	2	3	4

(continued)

Constructive Praising Critique Form

5. Was more of this behavior encouraged?   1   2   3   4
6. Was the receiver's value affirmed?   1   2   3   4
7. Was a feeling of closeness, caring, or   1   2   3   4
   sincerity established?

General comments and suggestions to improve this praising:

_____

_____

_____

■ Exercise 6.3

Far too often we do not receive the praisings we feel we deserve. Now is your opportunity to receive one. Think of an accomplishment that deserves praising. Answer the questions below as specifically as possible so that you will be able to explain the situation thoroughly to a partner. Ask a partner to deliver your praising, and then deliver his or her praising.

1. Identify the situation. What did you do?

   _____

   _____

2. Identify the specific behavior for which you feel you should have received praise.

   _____

   _____

3. Describe the impact of your behavior on the organization. Who benefited?

   _____

   _____

After you complete Exercise 6.2 and 6.3, reflect on the following questions:

1. How did it feel to give a praise?

   _____

2. How did it feel to receive a praise?

   _____

3. What did you find difficult about giving and receiving a praise?

   _____

   _____

6

Chapter Checkpoints

✓ Praising is a way of recognizing good performance and keeping it on track.

✓ Praises have more impact when they are immediate, genuine, and specific.

✓ Praise learners or trainees when their performance is approximately right.

✓ Praise seasoned employees when their performance is exactly right.

✓ When giving praises, avoid:

- "Yes, but,"
- Assigning more work,
- Gunnysacking.

✓ When you give praises:

- Tell the employee what he or she did right.
- Tell the employee how you feel about his or her behavior.
- Pause to allow the praising to be felt.
- Encourage the employee to do more of the same.
- Reaffirm that you value the employee and his or her performance.

7 | Constructive Criticism

This chapter will help you to:

- Understand why reprimands are necessary at times.
- See why some reprimands are ineffective.
- Deliver constructive criticism.
- Manage reactions to reprimands.

Ryan O'Leary is a mechanical engineer for DesignTech Corporation. Recently he was called in for a meeting with his division manager, Lech Sjokowski. Ryan has been sensing that Lech isn't happy with a design project he has been working on for six months. To date Ryan hasn't been given any feedback. He walks into Lech's office, nervous and anticipating the worst.

Lech opens the meeting by saying, "Well, I called you in here because, as you know, I'm not happy with your performance." He continues with a long list of performance problems, using choice phrases such as "I don't like your attitude," "You're not even trying," "You've never done anything right," "Remember six months ago when I had to ask you to . . .," and "Your co-worker told me that . . . ." Ryan felt totally helpless. Lech concluded by saying, "If these issues aren't resolved in 30 days, you'll be fired."

Ryan left the meeting, and as he stormed down the hall toward his office he felt a sense of growing rage. He mumbled to himself, "What a setup! How can I do anything about my performance when I don't even really know what I did wrong?" As the day progressed and Ryan tried to make sense of the meeting, he became angrier. He was furious that Lech had waited so long to talk to him, that he had talked with his

co-workers about his performance, and that he felt that he never did anything right and wasn't even trying. How unfair it all seemed! He thought to himself, "Maybe I'll just quit, but first I'm going to get even." ■

Questions to Consider

1. What went wrong?

   _____

   _____

2. If you were Ryan, what might you do to get even and why?

   _____

   _____

3. What impact might this situation have on Ryan's performance?

   _____

   _____

4. If you were Ryan's manager, what would you have done differently?

   _____

   _____

This chapter will examine the elements of constructive criticism, another essential ingredient of good performance management. It is a skill that should be used frequently in coaching. Far too often it is avoided because of the discomfort associated with delivering criticism. Remember that when you provide employees with immediate and specific feedback, even when it is negative, you give them opportunities to improve. When you do not, you often set them up for continuing and increased failure, thus making your own job more difficult.

REPRIMANDING EMPLOYEES

While praising is important in keeping good performance on track, there will be times when it is necessary to point out errors and reprimand employees whose performance has slipped. You must communicate what expectation has not been met, its impact, and your expectations for future performance. Only when employees have a clear understanding of your expectations can they take corrective action and improve their performance.

Why Are Some Reprimands Ineffective?

You probably think of reprimands as being negative because of past experiences. Consequently, you may try to avoid reprimands. But when given properly, reprimands can be used as *positive* tools to get good performers back on track.

■ Exercise 7.1

Think of a time when you were reprimanded. The reprimand should be one that you felt was ineffective. What was the person's behavior toward you and how did you feel about it?

Describe behaviors that made the reprimand a negative experience.	What were your feelings or reactions to this reprimand?
_____	_____
_____	_____
_____	_____
_____	_____
_____	_____
_____	_____
_____	_____
_____	_____

Compare your responses in Exercise 7.1 to the list in Figure 7.1. See if any of your behaviors, feelings, or reactions are the same as the ones given there.

FIGURE 7.1 INEFFECTIVE REPRIMANDS

Behaviors Present	Feelings or Reactions
Attacking personally rather than focusing on behavior	Defensive
	Resentful
Reprimanding new learner when goal clarification or more direction is needed	Inadequate
	Angry
Gunnysacking—saving up a list of problems and dumping it on the person all at once	Focus is on feelings rather than on correcting behavior
Basing feedback on inference rather than on observed behavior; sender never "owned" the reprimand	Frustration
	Upset
Reprimanding employee for something that occurred long ago; reprimand is not well-timed	Decreased trust and communication
	Wanting to get even
Delivering the same reprimand over and over, even after the performance has been corrected	Demotivated
	Feeling of never being able to win

When you reprimand someone, you need to:

- Make the facts surrounding the reprimand clear.
- State what the reprimanded employee must do and why.
- Reaffirm your belief in the reprimanded employee.

When you follow these guidelines, the recipient of the reprimand will be able to focus on his or her own behavior, not on yours.

Exercise 7.2

Think back on your career and pull out the most difficult employee performance issue you can remember. Answer the following questions:

1. What was the performance problem?

_____

_____

2. How did you handle it?

_____

_____

3. What were the results?

_____

_____

4. If this situation were to occur again, would you handle it differently? If so, how? If not, why not?

_____

_____

HOW TO DELIVER CONSTRUCTIVE CRITICISM*

Once you learn how to give constructive criticism, you will find that you will be able to use it appropriately and effectively. Here are seven suggested steps, adapted from _Building One Minute Management Skills_ by Dr. Kenneth Blanchard.

1. Tell the employee what he or she did wrong; be specific.
Communicate in specific descriptive terms what the inappropriate behavior was.
Communicate the impact of the behavior on you, the department, or the organization.

2. Tell the employee how you feel about the behavior; be direct.

3. Pause for a moment to let the reprimand be felt by the employee.

4. Solicit input from the employee.
Ask for more information about why the problem occurred.
Ask for ideas on how the problem can be solved or corrected.

5. Clarify your expectations for future behavior.
If an acceptable solution comes from the employee, restate it.

6. Get agreement and commitment to future expectations.
Remind the employee how much you, the department, and the organization value him or her.
Validate the employee's worth by using examples of past positive behaviors.

-----

*These suggestions for delivering constructive criticism are adapted with the approval of Blanchard Training and Development, Inc., from THE ONE MINUTE MANAGER by Kenneth Blanchard, Ph.D., and Spencer Johnson, M.D. Copyright 1981, 1982 by Blanchard Family Partnership and Candle Communications Corp. By permission of William Morrow & Company, Inc.

7

Important Tips

- Before giving a reprimand, investigate the situation. Find out if there is a legitimate reason why the employee is not performing well.
- Never reprimand a learner. Instead, go back to review performance goals and objectives.
- Reprimand the specific behavior, not the person.
- Give a reprimand immediately if it is appropriate.
- Remember not to "gunnysack," or save up reprimands.
- Realize that at the conclusion of the reprimand, the reprimand is over. Don't keep going over old ground.

A typical constructive criticism session might sound like the one below.

1. Describe the behavior: "This morning you interrrupted me several times while I was trying to handle a customer problem. This made an already awkward situation even more difficult."

2. Describe how you feel about the behavior and its impact on the whole: "I was surprised by your behavior because I know you are usually very sensitive to our customers' needs."

3. Pause to allow the reprimand to be felt.

4. Solicit input from the employee: "How can we resolve this in the future?" or "Why did this happen?"

5. Clarify your expectations for future behavior: "In the future, please wait until I am finished with my customer before asking me questions."

6. Get agreement and commitment to future expectations: "Do we agree that this is a reasonable request?" or "May I have your commitment to carry out this request in the future?"

7. Reaffirm and validate the employee: "I know that in the past you have served our customers extremely well (give specifics), and I hope that you'll continue to do so in the future. Your hard work is certainly appreciated by everyone here."

Exercise 7.3

Think of a current employee performance problem and answer the questions that follow.

1. What is the performance problem (in behavioral terms)?

   _____

   _____

2. What is happening now, and what do you want to happen? What is the level of performance now, and what do you want the level of performance to be (in business terms)?

   _____

   _____

   _____

   _____

3. Brainstorm possible solutions for handling the situation.

   _____

   _____

   _____

   _____

Exercise 7.4

After answering the above questions, fill in the following script. Use the constructive criticism example on page 70 as a model.

1. Describe the behavior: _____

   _____

2. Describe how you feel about the behavior and its impact on the whole: _____

   _____

3. Pause to allow the reprimand to be felt.

4. Solicit input from the employee: _____

   _____

5. Clarify your expectations for future behavior: _____

   _____

6. Get agreement and commitment to future expectations: _____

   _____

7. Reaffirm and validate the employee: _____

   _____

■ **E x e r c i s e   7 . 5**

Select a partner to role-play in a constructive criticism session. Take turns criticizing and receiving reprimands.

Following your role-play, use the critique form below as a guide. Use the form below to measure your performance in both roles.

Constructive Criticism Critique Form

Key: 1—Not at all; 2—Somewhat; 3—Pretty much; 4—Yes.

1. Was the behavior for which criticism was given stated specifically and descriptively?	1	2	3	4
2. Were the sender's feelings about the behavior shared with the receiver?	1	2	3	4
3. Was the impact of the behavior on a project, individual, department, or organization stated?	1	2	3	4
4. Did the sender pause to let the reprimand sink in?	1	2	3	4
5. Did the sender of the criticism try to find out from the receiver why the behavior happened and how the problem could be resolved?	1	2	3	4
6. Were the sender's expectations for future behavior clarified, and were the receiver's suggestions incorporated into them?	1	2	3	4
7. Did the sender get agreement and commitment to future expectations?	1	2	3	4
8. Was the receiver's value reaffirmed by the sender?	1	2	3	4
9. Was a feeling of closeness, caring, and sincerity established?	1	2	3	4

General comments and suggestions to improve this constructive criticism:

_____

_____

_____

REACTIONS TO CRITICISM

Even when reprimands are carefully planned and communicated, they are sometimes extremely difficult for people to swallow. A number of possible reactions and feelings can arise. Your ability to cope with these reactions can affect whether the employee will want to alter behavior, and look to you for ongoing support. Figure 7.2 lists typical reactions to reprimands along with suggested techniques for resolving them.

FIGURE 7.2

Possible Reactions	Possible Feelings	Techniques for Resolution
Silence	Shock disbelief, anger, fear	Silence. Acknowledge difficulty of accepting criticism. Ask for thoughts.
Crying	Sadness, fear, disappointment, anger	Ask employee how he or she feels. State your empathy for the situation. Allow a few minutes for the employee to calm down. Acknowledge feelings that are exposed.
Rage, shouting, loss of self-control	Anger, hurt	Allow venting. State that you understand employee is angry; ask for confirmation. Avoid defensiveness. Allow employee to ask questions. Respond factually and specifically. Avoid "forced calm."
Terseness, directness	Indignant feelings, frustration	Allow venting. State that you will respond to questions one at a time. Use silence to allow employee to reflect on his or her statements.
Remorse, pleading, bargaining	Guilt, fear, disbelief	Acknowledge feelings. Reinforce determination to achieve results and implement decisions. Encourage discussion of next steps. Be very clear and direct.

Note that if at any time emotions are too intense for calm and rational dialogue, it is best to discontinue the meeting and suggest another time to continue.

7

Chapter Checkpoints

✓ Reprimands are a way of getting good performers back on track.

✓ Reprimands are ineffective when they are not immediate, specific, or focused on behavior.

✓ When you give constructive criticism:

- Tell the employee what he or she did wrong; be specific.
- Tell the employee how you feel about his or her behavior.
- Pause to let the reprimand be felt.
- Solicit input from the employee.
- Clarify expectations for future behavior.
- Get agreement on and commitment to future expectations.
- Reaffirm and validate the employee.

✓ Manage reactions to criticisms supportively and effectively.

8 | Coaching

This chapter will help you to:

- Apply effective coaching technique.
- Use the performance analysis model.
- Coach for improved performance.
- Develop performance improvement plans.

Part 1. Dina Torelli is a seasoned account representative working for the Performance Plus Consulting Company. For the first two years on the job she was a top performer. She was well-respected by peers, managers, and customers for her ability to acquire new accounts and take projects from start to finish. During this time, she worked for a manager who seldom gave her the praising she deserved. Instead, her manager continually assigned more work to her, only stopping long enough to tell her what she was doing wrong and criticizing her for not being able to complete all her work, which more than tripled in volume every six months.

Part 2. After two years, Dina became extremely frustrated with her situation. She requested a transfer within the company and was assigned to a new territory. Her personal goals were to develop new skills and to become a regional account manager. Unfortunately, Dina experienced much of her old frustration in the new position. Her new manager relied heavily on her existing skills and never seemed to have enough time to give her development opportunities.

Part 3. Four years passed, and Dina's performance suffered. Her frustration with her managers and the company began to surface in her everyday work. Her attendance was sporadic and her tardiness excessive. Her declining performance was evident to

peers, managers, and customers alike. Her new manager, Sally Artez, received numerous complaints about Dina's performance. Knowing about Dina's history with the company, Sally decided to ignore Dina's current performance problems. She justified this in saying, "It's just a passing phase. She'll be back on her feet in no time. We just need to give her a chance. She's too good to lose. She's one of our top performers."

Part 4. Sally continued to supervise Dina in this manner and Dina's problems at work became progressively worse. Sally spent an increasing amount of her time putting out fires that Dina had started with her peers, customers, and other managers. Dina's consistently poor performance ultimately began to reflect on Sally's performance. The regional director told Sally to "do something" about Dina. Sally thought to herself, "I don't know what to do. I've tried everything!" ■

■ Questions to Consider

1. Identify what went wrong with the management of Dina's performance?

Part 1: _____

_____

Part 2: _____

_____

Part 3: _____

_____

Part 4: _____

_____

2. Summarize how poor management affected Dina's performance over time.

Part 1: _____

_____

Part 2: _____

_____

Part 3: _____

_____

Part 4: _____

_____

3. What do you think Sally should do about Dina's performance problems now?

_____

_____

4. What performance problems might have been prevented or resolved with appropriate coaching?

_____

_____

5. If you were Dina's manager, how would you have managed her performance? What type of coaching would you suggest at each part of the case study, and what results would you expect to achieve?

Part 1: _____

_____

_____

Part 2: _____

_____

_____

Part 3: _____

_____

_____

Part 4: _____

_____

_____

8

WHAT IS COACHING?

Coaching is the key to developing people. It consists of frequent, specific feedback intended to raise the level of performance. It is used for acknowledging good performance and for communicating the need for improvement. Coaching need not be limited to performance that is grossly inadequate or at the height of perfection. A great deal of coaching can be used effectively when an employee's performance is very good but could still be improved.

Coaching has many important applications and functions.

- Providing performance feedback to employees (praising, reprimanding, enhancing performance).

- Expanding or developing an employee's existing skills (giving assignments, providing development opportunities, training for improved performance).

- Consulting with an employee on obstacles to goals and objectives (addressing motivational issues, providing referral resources).

- Preparing an employee for promotion or increased responsibility (career development discussions).

- Confronting an employee about performance that consistently falls below expectations or that deteriorates (reviewing implications of poor performance; suggesting alternative avenues, such as transfer, discharge, or meaningful employment outside the organization, if appropriate).

PERFORMANCE ANALYSIS MODEL

One way of looking at performance and identifying coaching needs is through the performance analysis model.*

In this model, employees fall into one of the following five categories:

1. *Workhorses.* People on whom you can rely and who get the job done. Their potential is moderate, but their performance is high.

---

*The Performance Analysis Model (Figure 8.1) is based on J. William Pfeiffer and Leonard D. Goodstein, *The 1984 Annual: Developing Human Resources*, San Diego, CA: Pfeiffer & Company, 1984. Used with permission.

2. *Stars.* People who have high potential as well as high performance.

3. *Trainees.* People who are new employees or learners. They have potential to perform well with training and support.

4. *Problem children.* People who have high potential but who do not perform well, even after support. Managers often spend too much time with these employees, getting caught in what is known as the "savior syndrome" in their desire to avoid conflict.

5. *Deadwood.* People who are nonproductive and have low potential and low performance. These people are often known as the "quit-and-stay" type—employees who show up for work in body only. In a tight economy, organizations usually divest themselves of this group.

Performance Analysis Model

The diagram on page 79 illustrates this model. The model can be used to give you general direction. It can be extremely effective in examining performance by specific task or goal, rather than lumping an employee in one particular box for all goals.

■ Exercise 8.1

Based on what you already know about the different applications for coaching, describe the type of coaching you would recommend for each group in the performance analysis model.

Star: _____

_____

Workhorse: _____

_____

Deadwood: _____

_____

Trainee: _____

_____

Problem child: _____

_____

The following table lists some suggested applications for Exercise 8.1.

Type of Employee	Coaching Application
Star:	Praise to keep performance on track. Educate to expand skills. Sponsor/mentor for increased responsibility.
Workhorse:	Praise to keep performance on track. If the person wants to expand skills or be promoted, the coach can use educating, sponsoring, and mentoring.
Deadwood:	Confront (up or out). Coach to problem—skills, motivation, etc. (avoid savior syndrome).
Trainee:	Train or educate to move to workhorse or star.
Problem child:	Control (up or out). Coach to problem to increase performance—often a motivation problem (avoid savior syndrome).

Remember to use your management time wisely; spend time where you will get results, and avoid the savior syndrome.

■ **E x e r c i s e   8 . 2**

Consider the employees who report to you, then plot them in the performance analysis model box below. You may find that they fall into different boxes if you examine their skill and commitment to each goal, task, or situation separately. Next consider the type of coaching that may be helpful to them. Write their names, the task at hand, and your ideas in the chart on page 82.

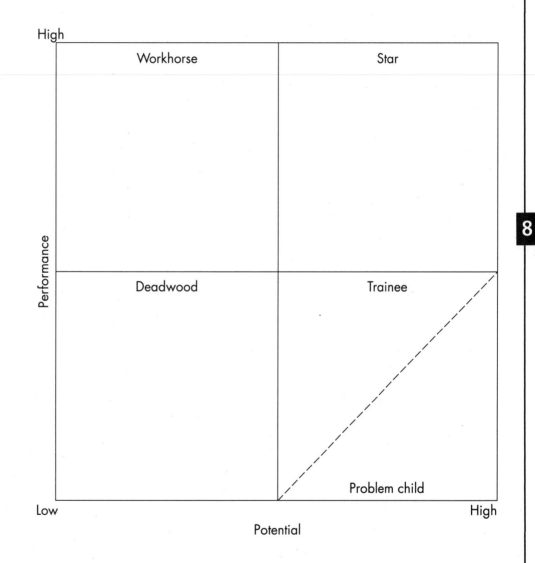

Share your responses with a partner to see whether he or she agrees with your assessment and to get some additional feedback on your coaching ideas.

EMPLOYEE PERFORMANCE ANALYSIS CHART

Employee Name(s)	Tasks(s)	Ideas for Coaching

8

COACHING FOR IMPROVED PERFORMANCE

As you track performance, it is important to consider whether patterns of behavior suggest performance problems. As you become aware of a performance problem, you should ask yourself the following questions:

1. Does the employee know what is expected of him or her?
2. Are there obstacles beyond the employee's control?
3. Does the employee lack some essential skill, knowledge, training, or experience?
4. Is there a motivational issue involved?
5. Is the performance problem due to interpersonal style or skills?

After asking yourself these questions, gather all pertinent information regarding the specific performance problem. The coaching model on page 84 addresses most performance problems.

A step-by-step example of the coaching model in action is seen below.

1. Review status of objective: "As you know, a goal for our company and for every individual employee this year is to strive for 100 percent on-time delivery to our customers."
2. Talk about performance: "On three occasions this week, you have been 20 minutes late for work. In the past, however, I've been able to count on you to be on time."
3. Identify how the employee's performance presents problems or obstacles: "When you were late, it caused a delay in our production schedule. This delay affects our ability to meet our on-time goal and improve our service to our customers."
4. Solicit input: "Can you tell me why you have had trouble getting here on time this week?"
5. Discuss changes: "In the future, I expect you to be here and at work on time (e.g., 8:00 A.M.) every morning."
6. Clarify how you can help: "Is there any way I can help you in meeting this objective?"
7. Agree on action plan: "Can we agree that from now on you'll make an extra effort to be on time?"

8

8

Coaching Model

1. **Review status of objective.** Review the performance objective to be discussed.

2. **Talk about performance.** Assess performance for areas that can be improved. Use *specific* job examples that highlight areas of poor performance. Provide balanced feedback. Focus on the action or behavior to be improved, not the person.

3. **Identify how the employee's performance presents problems or obstacles.** Specify how performance affects the employee's ability to accomplish the particular goal or objective involved.

4. **Solicit input.** Understand the employee's point of view. Be sure to ask for the employee's assessment of the problem.

5. **Discuss changes.** Discuss specific goals, objectives, and time-tables for accomplishment or improvement.

6. **Clarify how you can help.** The employee should "own" the problem and solutions. You offer support and assistance.

7. **Agree on action plan.** Clarify and gain agreement on expectations for future performance.

8. **Schedule follow-up.** Establish definite review points for monitoring progress and providing feedback.

9. **Reaffirm and validate.** Be sure that the employee is left with a feeling of self-worth and ability to contribute to the organization.

   Note: Depending on the severity of the problem or the frequency of coaching given in the past for the same problem, some optional and additional steps may be called for. Always remember to close with reaffirmation and validation.

a) Discuss implications of continued performance. An employee should be aware of the potential consequences of failure to improve.

b) Documentation. Document the discussion and provide the employee with a copy of the documentation to ensure a common understanding.

   Before using either of these latter steps, seek guidance from your manager or human resources personnel. Many companies have varying and specific policies related to these matters.

8. Schedule follow-up: "Let's get together next Friday afternoon to talk about how things are going."

9. Reaffirm and validate: "You've been one of our top performers in the past, and we need you on our team."

■ Exercise 8.3

Describe an employee performance problem within your work unit. This should be different from the problem you chose previously for constructive criticism. It is important that this issue be tied directly to at least one of the employee's performance goals. Be brief but specific in your description. (If you do not have any issues, describe a situation where someone is performing well now but with your support could be performing at an even higher level. Modify the coaching process accordingly.)

Description of Performance Problem:

_____

_____

_____

Using the outline provided below, develop a coaching script for improving the performance problem you just described. Then use the critique form on page 86 to role-play your situation with a partner and solicit feedback. Remember, feedback should be constructive and should follow the guidelines presented earlier. After the first role-play and critique, reverse roles with your partner.

1. Review status of objective: _____

_____

2. Talk about performance: _____

_____

3. Identify how the employee's performance presents problems or obstacles: _____

_____

4. Solicit input: _____

_____

5. Discuss changes: _____

_____

8

6. Clarify how you can help: _____

7. Agree on action plan: _____

8. Schedule follow-up: _____

9. Reaffirm and validate: _____

Coaching Critique Form

1. Was the objective reviewed and restated? _____

2. Was the specific performance problem discussed appropriately? _____

3. Were the problems or obstacles created by the employee's performance problem identified? _____

4. Was input from the employee solicited? _____

5. Were changes discussed? _____

6. Was the supervisor's help or support clarified? _____

7. Were action plans developed and agreed upon? _____

8. Was a schedule of follow-up or review established? _____

9. Was the employee reaffirmed or validated? _____

Additional feedback: _____
Strengths: _____
Improvements needed: _____
Areas for development: _____

WRITTEN IMPROVEMENT PLANS

In some situations it may be necessary to move from less formal coaching and feedback techniques to a written improvement plan. Such a plan formally documents the level of performance and steps to be taken prior to an annual performance appraisal at the end of the review period.

THE IMPROVEMENT PLAN MEETING

To prepare for the meeting:

1. Collect specific, recent examples of the performance problem.
2. Observe the performance in question.
3. Choose an appropriate time, place, and environment for the meeting, ensuring no interruptions.

Conducting the meeting:

1. State the purpose of the meeting.
2. Describe current performance results using coaching and feedback guidelines.
3. Elicit information about causes of the problem from the employee.
4. Describe expected performance.
5. Discuss possible solutions—what does the employee need to do to close the "performance gap"?
6. Discuss what assistance or support is needed from you, the manager.
7. Review the consequences of failure to improve performance.
8. Set a date to review progress.
9. Reaffirm and validate.

Following the meeting:

1. Document the discussion and provide the employee with a copy to ensure a common understanding of expectations. In some cases, a performance improvement contract may be recommended.
2. Monitor ongoing performance.
   - If performance does not show improvement, you may need to take progressive disciplinary action. Before taking such a step, it is imperative to speak with your manager as well as your human resources personnel to familiarize yourself with company policy on such matters.

Exercise 8.4

Consider the performance problem you covered in Exercise 8.3. For the purpose of this exercise, assume that the problem still has not been corrected and that you feel a need to develop a formal performance improvement plan. Prepare, conduct, and follow up on an improvement plan meeting based on what you just learned. As this is a simulated situation, end your follow-up process with your documentation or performance contract.

Role-play your situation with a partner. Each of you should take turns experiencing the roles of employee and manger, then receive feedback on your performances.

8

Chapter Checkpoints

✓ Coaching can be used to:
- Give performance feedback.
- Educate and develop.
- Counsel.
- Sponsor or mentor.
- Confront.

✓ When you coach for improved performance:
- Review status of objective.
- Talk about performance.
- Identify how the employee's performance presents problems or obstacles.
- Solicit input.
- Discuss changes.
- Clarify how you can help.
- Agree on action plan.
- Schedule follow-up.
- Reaffirm and validate.

✓ Improvement plans document the current level of performance and identify steps to be taken for corrective action.

9 Progress Reviews

This chapter will help you to:

- Prepare for progress reviews.
- Conduct progress reviews.
- Learn how to follow up on progress reviews.

Flora Gonzalez is a seasoned social worker for Neighborhoods United. She has just learned about a new performance management system to be used throughout her organization. It is time to give her first progress review, so she dutifully informs one of her subordinates, Penny Pearlman, that they will be meeting tomorrow to discuss her performance. Penny, fairly new to the organization and not at all sure what this meeting will entail, arrives in Flora's office the next day filled with apprehension. She has had no prior feedback on her performance and does not have the slightest idea what her manager really thinks of her or the work she does.

Flora begins the review by restating all the goals and objectives originally established in Penny's performance plan. Penny's head begins to spin as she tries to remember all the goals being rattled off.

Flora then says to Penny, "You've been doing a great job. I can't think of anything you need to improve on. In fact, because of your excellent performance I'm now going to assign you the job of team leader. That's all I have to say for now. Keep up the great work."

Penny is flabbergasted. She had walked in wondering if she would have a job next week, knowing full well that she was falling behind in some of her goals. Now she was promoted before she felt well-grounded in her current job. She would have liked her boss to have been more specific and to have coached her in some of the areas where she felt she needed some development. But since Flora had just painted her as the perfect employee, Penny felt it would be in her best interest to say nothing.

As she returns to her office, Penny begins to wonder what it would mean to be a team leader. Does she now have to do it all—her job plus this new one? How can she possibly be successful? What skills will she need that she does not have now? Will she triumph or fail? ∎

Questions to Consider

1. What went wrong with Penny's progress review?

_____

_____

2. How do you think the review will affect Penny's performance now and over time?

_____

_____

3. If you were Penny's manager, how would you have conducted the progress review? What would you have done differently?

_____

_____

WHAT ARE PROGRESS REVIEWS?

Interim coaching provides _informal_, routine, and ongoing feedback. Progress reviews on the other hand, are conducted quarterly and provide a _formal_ opportunity to discuss overall performance results. Progress review meetings allow you to summarize informal feedback and are vital to managing performance. As in any good coaching situation, you must prepare for these meetings, conduct them well, and provide whatever feedback is necessary.

The overall purpose of a progress review is to:

- Progress toward goals and objectives established in performance and development plans.
- Review objectives and plans in light of business changes.
- Discuss needed changes, revisions, or additions to the performance and development plan.
- Make plans for improvement, if necessary. If progress is insufficient, you must determine what the problems are, solicit the employee's perspective and suggested solutions, and utilize appropriate coaching skills. In some cases a formal improvement plan will need to be developed.

PREPARING FOR PROGRESS REVIEWS

First of all, you'll need all pertinent information at hand. Establishing a drop file for each of your employees in which you collect performance data over time (e.g., positive, negative, and neutral) is a convenient and objective way to track individual performance.

Plan to review each employee thoroughly on a quarterly basis to avoid the anxiety brought on by a yearly review. When a quarterly review system is in place, the manager has collected factual data throughout the year to use in objective performance reviews. By the time the annual review comes up, (this will be covered in Chapter 10) the employee on the receiving end experiences no great surprises, because much of what is discussed during the annual review is merely a summation of prior formal and informal feedback discussions.

You should take several steps before holding a progress review meeting:

- Inform the employee about the meeting, agenda, and purpose at least one week in advance.
- Advise the employee to be prepared to discuss recommended changes to the current performance and development plan.
- Review the status of your department's business plans, the employee's development activities, and his or her performance. As necessary, draft a list of changes needed on the performance and development plan. Be prepared to discuss them.
- If the initial performance plan is still valid, use the meeting to give the employee feedback on current performance.
- Schedule enough uninterrupted time based on the type of changes to be made, the level of employee performance, and the amount of information you need to discuss. Be sure your meeting room is comfortable and private.

As you prepare for the progress review, ask yourself the following questions:

1. If changes are recommended, consider:
   - What changes in the company business plan have occurred? How have these changes altered the employee's objectives and the performance plan?
   - What development activities, if any, will the employee need as a result of changes in the business plan and the individual performance plan?

2. If performance needs improvement, consider:
   - How is the employee's current performance not meeting the requirements of the job?
   - What action can I take to assist or support the employee in improving performance? What other resources are available?
   - What action should the employee take to improve his or her own performance?

- How significant is the unacceptable performance? Is it in a critical area of the employee's job? Does it affect other employees or customers?
- What will I do if performance continues at an unacceptable level?

3. If performance is superior or outstanding, consider:
   - How is the employee's performance exceeding the requirements of the job?
   - What actions can I take to keep the job challenging and interesting for the employee?
   - What plans do I need to make in order to reward this employee for his or her superior performance?
   - Are there projects with higher levels of responsibility in which the employee would excel?
   - Are others learning from this employee's example? How can this performer teach others?
   - Are there promotional opportunities for this employee?

Exercise 9.1

Choose one of your employees and consider his or her current performance and development plan. Write down the key goals and objectives of his or her job, including both performance expectations and development activities. Prepare to give the employee feedback on performance to date using the performance and development objectives as a basis for discussion. Consider both coaching needs and any changes in plans that may be appropriate. Use the Progress Review Summary Form on page 96 to prepare this progress review.

The best test of your performance review preparation is to make sure the review measures progress toward goals set at previous performance and development planning meetings. If the performance review covers those agreed upon goals, you have good basis for the review meeting.

CONDUCTING PROGRESS REVIEW MEETINGS: GUIDELINES

1. State the purpose of the discussion.
2. Restate and review the status of each objective.
3. Exchange views about the plan and provide feedback on the employee's performance progress to date.

Progress Review Summary Form

Performance goals and objectives (include measurements/standards)	Actual performance results (state in measurable terms)
1.	
2.	
3.	
4.	
5.	

Development activities	Actual activities or results
1.	
2.	
3.	

4. Provide specific examples of performance to date.

5. Identify outstanding accomplishments or performance gaps.

6. If there are performance gaps, specify:
   a. How performance is not meeting expectations.
   b. What aspects of performance are not acceptable.

7. Solicit the employee's assessment whenever a performance problem is evident. Understand his or her point of view and ideas for resolution.

8. If coaching is required to improve performance, be specific, and use appropriate procedures for communicating.

9. Discuss expected changes.

10. Clarify how you can help.

11. Work with the employee, soliciting feedback to reach agreement on a plan of action.

12. Review the development plan; discuss progress to date and any changes that need to be made.

13. Summarize your discussion; schedule a follow-up meeting.

There are several important issues to keep in mind when conducting progress review meetings.

Review one goal or objective at a time. First, focus on the performance plan, goal by goal, and then use the same process to discuss the development plan.

Present a balanced review. Because you want to present a balanced review where people feel supported, you may elect to discuss performance goals out of order. Start off on a positive note by focusing on an area of performance where the employee does well. Avoid the downward spiral created by saving the worst for last. Instead, create balance in the review wherever possible. Place the discussion of goals where improvement is needed between areas where there has been peformance success. Remember to keep the discussion of each goal separate.

Make necessary changes in performance and development plans. It is important to remember that performance and development plans are not fixed in stone. Through the course of interim coaching and progress reviews, you or your employee may see where plans need to be altered. When this occurs, follow these suggested steps:

- Pencil in any changes to the original plan and date them.
- Be sure the changes are clear to the employee.
- Make sure both of you know what effect the change will have on the rest of the performance objectives and on the way results will be measured.
- Consider what effect the revisions may have, if any, on the development plan. New performance objectives may trigger the need for new development activities.
- Continue to use the revised plan as your working document for the rest of the review period.
- Be alert to changes in priorities, new assignments, and new deadlines and what effect they may have on your employee's performance plan. Be ready to make adjustments to the plans and discuss them when necessary.

Exercise 9.2

Refer to the form that you filled out in Exercise 9.1. Now conduct a progress review meeting using the progress review guidelines just discussed. Choose a partner to play the role of your employee and solicit his or her feedback on your performance following the review. After receiving feedback, allow your partner an opportunity to practice his or her review skills by reversing roles and repeating the same steps.

Your partner will be the main source of feedback for this exercise. Feedback should be based on the progress review guidelines. Constructive coaching skills also should be applied.

FOLLOWING UP PROGRESS REVIEWS

It is essential to remember that formal progress reviews need to occur every 90 days in a year-long review cycle. Ample ongoing informal feedback and interim coaching should take place between formal reviews. Figure 9.1 depicts the progress review cycle.

Exercise 9.3

Refer to the Performance Management Planning and Tracking Chart on page 100. List your employees and chart your performance management plans. Be sure to include the initial performance and development planning session, quarterly progress reviews, the annual performance appraisal, and performance planning time prior to the start of the next cycle. Interim coaching may be included in this chart and should be recorded at the time it is given.

9

FIGURE 9.1   CYCLE OF PROGRESS REVIEWS

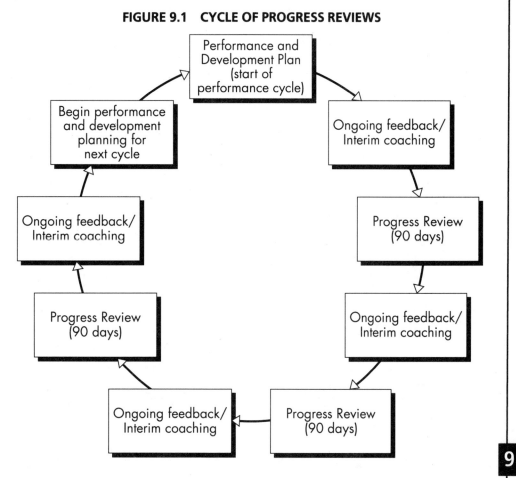

Performance Management Planning and Tracking Chart

Manager _____

Current Staffing Level _____   Projected Staffing Level _____

	July	Aug.	Sept.	Oct.	Nov.	Dec.	Jan.	Feb.	Mar.	Apr.	May	June
Employee Name:												
Employee Name:												
Employee Name:												
Employee Name:												
Employee Name:												
Employee Name:												

Chapter Checkpoints

✓ Progress reviews are *formal* meetings to:

- Discuss an employee's progress based on established performance and development plans.

- Update performance and development plans.

✓ To prepare for progress reviews:

- Inform the employee about the meeting and agenda a week ahead of time.

- Be prepared to discuss performance results and suggested changes to the performance plan.

✓ To conduct a performance review meeting, follow these guidelines:

- Restate and review the status of objectives.

- Exchange views about the plan.

- Talk about both good and bad performance.

- Identify how the employee's performance presents problems or obstacles or contributes to meeting objectives.

- Solicit employee input. Provide appropriate feedback and coaching.

- Discuss expected changes, as appropriate.

- Clarify how you can help.

- Agree on mutual action plans.

- Summarize the meeting; schedule a follow-up meeting.

✓ Progress review meetings should be scheduled every 90 days within an annual review cycle, with intermittent ongoing coaching.

10 | Annual Appraisals and Reviews

This chapter will help you to:

- Prepare and conduct annual performance appraisals and development reviews.

It was Friday at 4 P.M. at Futures Biotech, Inc. Abner Conroy, a research and development manager, had just received a memo from the human resources director reminding him that his annual employee evaluations were delinquent. He had forgotten all about them.

He saw Hisae Koizumi, one of his employees, bustling by his office. She was near completion of a big research assignment, which was due by 5 o'clock that afternoon. Abner ran after her and said, "We have to meet in five minutes to discuss your performance review. It's overdue." Hisae was surprised and flustered because she wanted to finish her project on time, but Abner was the boss.

Hisae entered Abner's office five minutes later. Abner was totally unprepared and proceeded in his usual monologue style, subjecting Hisae to a one-way subjective evaluation of her performance and answering phone calls intermittently. Often losing his train of thought, he went on and on, talking generally about what she did and did not do, never getting specific or backing up his comments with documentation. Any specifics given were based on events that occurred over the previous month, as if the prior eleven months were simply too far in the distant past to bother remembering. At times, Abner's evaluation was far from factual, but Abner did not give Hisae the opportunity to respond to any of his comments. Hisae was extremely proud of her development activities, and these were not even mentioned.

Abner summarized his review with sharp criticism of Hisae's performance and ended their meeting promptly at 4:30 P.M. Abner knew that Hisae had always been a hard worker and was recognized for her scientific skills and abilities, but it went against his management style to let his employees know how valued they were. He was afraid that they would lose respect for him and try to undermine his authority.

Hisae left the review surprised as well as terribly disappointed. She wondered why she had bothered doing all that she had for the company. No one even noticed her effort. As a result of her outstanding reputation in her field, she had had many invitations from other companies but had declined them because of her sense of loyalty to Futures Biotech. Now she was left wondering if she should respond to the next invitation that came her way. ■

Questions to Consider

1. What do you think went wrong in the preparation stage of this review?

_____

_____

2. What do you think went wrong during the delivery of the performance appraisal and development review?

_____

_____

3. What impact do you think Hisae's review will have on her future performance and/or emotional commitment to the company?

_____

_____

4. If you were Abner, what would you have done differently in the preparation and review stages?

Preparation: _____

_____

Review: _____

_____

WHAT ARE ANNUAL PERFORMANCE APPRAISALS AND DEVELOPMENT REVIEWS?

The third and final phase of the performance management cycle is the annual performance appraisal and development review. It provides an opportunity to compare overall performance results with the objectives and expectations established in the performance plan.

The annual review is an opportunity to summarize formally the ongoing dialogue between you and your employee about the employee's performance. You will do the following at the annual review:

1. Review annual performance results compared with expectations.
2. Identify accomplishments and areas needing improvement.
3. Review the results of development activities.
4. Discuss significant factors affecting job performance (positively or negatively).
5. Assign objective specific and overall performance ratings.
6. Summarize the review on a performance and development form.

10

PREPARING FOR ANNUAL PERFORMANCE APPRAISALS AND DEVELOPMENT REVIEWS

After you review and analyze your employee's accomplishments, weaknesses, and performance over a full review cycle (i.e., one year), you and the employee are ready to have a performance appraisal discussion. As with other performance management meetings, it is imperative to prepare for and conduct the meeting in a professional and objective manner. Much of your ability to do this well rests upon your documentation of performance over the year.

When preparing for annual performance and development reviews focus on the following key areas prior to the annual review meeting.

- Inform the employee about the meeting and its purpose and agenda at least one week in advance. Ask him or her to prepare a written self-evaluation on his or her accomplishments or, at the very least, be prepared to discuss them. Be sure to schedule enough time—anywhere between one and two hours per review.
- Hold a pre-appraisal meeting with the employee to conduct a final check on objectives and to discuss the employee's input and your appraisal.
- Complete an appraisal form. Include the following on the form:
  - a. The employee's accomplishments, including the degree of success achieved compared with the objectives in the performance plan. Be objective and specific.
  - b. Additional accomplishments that were not part of the plan and their effect on overall performance.
  - c. Comments on the results of development activities.
- Review the appraisal with the appropriate parties ahead of time. Ensuring that your performance appraisal of an employee will be supported and approved is an important step prior to your discussion with the employee. Reviews often influence merit raises, work assignments, promotions, and so forth, which may require your manager's support and signature.

As you prepare for any performance review, consider the following key areas and related questions:

1. Preparation: Have I prepared well?
2. Documentation: Do I have sufficient factual information?

3. **Interim coaching:** Have I provided ongoing coaching and support, and is there more I can provide?

4. **Objectivity:** Am I focusing on behavior, not personality?

5. **Balance:** Have I balanced strengths/weaknesses?

6. **Agreement:** Am I prepared to listen to the employee and gain agreement on each objective before moving on?

7. **Reaffirmation:** Am I prepared to provide ongoing motivation through affirmation?

CONDUCTING ANNUAL PERFORMANCE APPRAISALS AND DEVELOPMENT REVIEWS

Conducting an annual performance review is very similar to conducting a progress review. The key guidelines are summarized here.

1. Review each performance objective and discuss your appraisal of the degree of success achieved. Be sure to solicit the employee's perspective of his or her performance. Review one objective at a time. It is important to try to reach agreement with the employee on your assessment before moving on to the next objective. If you do not, the employee's ability to focus in on and hear the rest of the review may be limited.

2. Discuss your conclusions about the employee's overall performance. Your conclusions and overall evaluation of performance are based on the degree of achievement of the objectives described in the performance plan. Be sure your evaluation is objective, based on measurable standards, and defendable.

3. After completing your discussion of the performance objectives, turn to the development plans and review them one by one in a similar fashion. They include the knowledge, skills, or abilities to be developed that you and your employee identified at the beginning of the review cycle on the development plan. (Note: Some companies choose not to include the results of development activities as part of the overall performance rating.)

4. Be sure you have communicated your review clearly. Give the employee an opportunity to discuss and ask questions about the content of the appraisal.

5. Once all issues are resolved to your satisfaction, give the employee an opportunity to record any comments, including disagreements, on the appraisal form.

10

6. Both you and the employee should sign and date the appraisal form. If required by policy or recommended for communication purposes, review the completed form with your immediate manager. If minor changes are necessary, inform the employee, modify the form, and have the employee initial the revised form. If major changes are necessary, complete a new appraisal form and include appropriate signatures. Your immediate manager may also want to sign and date the appraisal form.

7. Establish a date for the next performance and development planning discussion. At that meeting, you and the employee will plan next year's performance and development objectives.

■ Exercise 10.1

A sample performance appraisal and development review form in four sections is shown on pp. 109–113. Choose one of your current employees as the target of this review and complete the sample. The form includes its own instructions. Follow them as you proceed.

The purpose of this review is to evaluate and discuss an employee's overall performance. It should be based on expectations established in the performance and development plan for the current performance cycle. Assessments should be objective, thorough, and well understood by the employee in order to reward past performance and affect future performance. The performance and development review is the culmination of the ongoing performance management process which began with setting objectives and measurement criteria and continued throughout the year-long performance cycle with interim coaching and progress reviews. Doing this well is one of the most significant contributions any manager can make.

**Performance Appraisal and
Development Review Form**

EMPLOYEE NAME: _____

TITLE: _____

OFFICE/DEPARTMENT/DIVISION: _____

MEASUREMENT PERIOD: ___/___/___ TO ___/___/___

DATES OF PROGRESS REVIEWS: 1) _____, 2) _____, 3) _____

Section I: PERFORMANCE APPRAISAL

Objectives:
Describe the major performance objectives listed in the employee's performance plan. Be sure to state any modifications or revisions to the original plan and how these might affect performance. Indicate the weight of each objective or the percent of the total job responsibilities. The sum of all objectives should be no greater than 100 percent.

Results:
Document the results achieved using specific examples of performance. Rate the results in (   ), using the rating scale below. Refer to the relevant measurement criteria as indicated on the performance plan to support your rating.

Performance Appraisal Rating Scale: Definitions

(5) Superior	Results achieved *significantly exceed* job requirements.
(4) Commendable	Results achieved *consistently exceed* job requirements.
(3) Satisfactory	Results achieved *consistently meet* job requirements and may exceed them in some areas.
(2) Needs improvement	Results achieved *generally fall short of* job requirements.
(1) Unsatisfactory	Results achieved *fall short of* minimum job requirements.

Operational/business objectives:

1. Performance Objective:	Weight (%)
Summary of Results:	Rating ( )
2. Performance Objective:	Weight (%)
Summary of Results:	Rating ( )

10

Section I: *(concluded)*

3. Performance Objective: Weight
                                                   (%)

   Summary of Results: Rating
                                                   ( )

4. Performance Objective: Weight
                                                   (%)

   Summary of Results: Rating
                                                   ( )

5. Performance Objective: Weight
                                                   (%)

   Summary of Results: Rating
                                                   ( )

6. Performance Objective: Weight
                                                   (%)

   Summary of Results: Rating
                                                   ( )

10

Section II: OVERALL PERFORMANCE RATING AND SUMMARY

Summary comments:

Summarize the overall performance for the entire performance cycle or evaluation period. (Note: Also consider the following performance characteristics: job knowledge, planning and organization, leadership and people management, critical thinking and decision making, communications, initiative and creativity, dependability, adaptability, relating to others.)

10

Section III: INDIVIDUAL DEVELOPMENT PLAN REVIEW

A. Development plan review
Review the results of the employee's development activities as described on the most recent individual development plan. Identify specific knowledge and/or skills that were developed or strengthened as a result of those activities.

B. Strengths and development needs
Based on both the performance and development review, describe the knowledge, skills, and/or abilities that were most useful to the individual in achieving results. Describe at least two or three of these strengths. Also identify the specific knowledge, skills, and/or abilities that, if enhanced, would contribute most to improved performance. (These should be incorporated into development plans for the next review cycle.)

Strengths	Development needs

Section IV: COMMENTS AND SIGNATURES

I have reviewed this evaluation and discussed it with my manager. My signature indicates that I have been advised of my performance status, and it does not necessarily imply that I agree or disagree with this evaluation.

_____ __/__/__
MANAGER   DATE

_____ __/__/__
NEXT LEVEL MANAGER   DATE

_____ __/__/__
EMPLOYEE   DATE

Employee comments:

Additional management comments:

10

■ **E x e r c i s e   1 0 . 2**

Using the review you prepared in Exercise 10.1, find a partner to play the role of your employee. Conduct a review based on the guidelines discussed in the chapter. Ask your partner to be realistic when reacting to your review.

Because your partner may not be familiar with your employee's role, you may need to spend a few minutes to familiarize him or her with the job you are evaluating. Describe the key objectives and overall nature of the work. (This is a good way to test how clearly your goals have been written.) Do not discuss your review of the employee's actual performance prior to the role-play.

Once you have completed the initial role-play, reverse roles and repeat the process. This will give your partner an opportunity to practice his or her performance review skills as well.

10

Chapter Checkpoints

✓ The overall purpose of annual performance appraisals and development reviews is to measure annual performance against objectives established in the performance plan.

✓ To prepare for an annual review:

- Inform your employee about the meeting and its purpose at least one week in advance.

- Complete the appraisal form.

- Discuss the appraisal form with your manager ahead of time.

✓ Follow these guidelines for conducting performance appraisals and development reviews:

- Review each objective and measurement criteria.

- Discuss your performance evaluation and rating. Gain agreement. (Review one objective at a time.)

- Discuss your overall evaluation and rating. Gain agreement.

- Discuss development plan and results.

- Check to make sure your evaluation has been clearly understood throughout the review process.

- Ask the employee for comments and record them.

- Sign and date the appraisal form.

- Set a date for the next performance and development planning discussion.

Post-Test

You have just taken another step in your professional development by completing *Effective Performance Management.*

This post-test is provided to reinforce the material you have just covered. If you have difficulty with any questions, go back to the book to review key concepts.

1. What is performance management?

_____

_____

2. Why is performance management essential?

_____

_____

3. List the key stages of performance management.

_____

_____

_____

4. What is the difference between a goal and an objective?

_____

_____

_____

5. To test how well your objectives are written, use the acronym SMART, which stands for _____, _____, _____, _____, and _____.

6. What are performance and development plans?

_____

_____

7. When should performance and development planning be conducted?

_____

8. Describe the roles and responsibilities in the performance planning process for the following:

Manager/Supervisor: _____

_____

_____

Employee: _____

_____

_____

9. What is interim coaching? How and when should it be used?

_____

_____

_____

10. List guidelines for effective performance management.

_____

_____

_____

11. Why and when should you praise employees for their performance?

_____

_____

_____

12. List the steps involved in giving praises.

_____

_____

_____

_____

13. Why and when should you give constructive criticism on performance?

_____

_____

_____

14. List the steps involved in giving constructive criticism.

_____

_____

_____

_____

_____

_____

_____

15. In what ways can coaching skills be used to develop people?

_____

_____

_____

16. List the steps involved in coaching for improved performance.

_____

_____

_____

_____

_____

_____

_____

_____

17. What are progress reviews? How often should they be conducted?

_____

_____

_____

18. List the steps involved in conducting progress reviews.

_____

_____

_____

_____

_____

_____

_____

19. What is an annual review and why should it be conducted?

_____
_____
_____

20. List the steps involved in conducting annual performance appraisals and development reviews.

_____
_____
_____
_____
_____
_____
_____
_____
_____

Suggested Solutions

Chapter Two

Exercise 2.1 (Page 14)

1. T	5. F	9. T
2. T	6. T	10. F
3. F	7. F	11. T
4. T	8. F	12. T

Exercise 2.2 (Page 14)

1. **G.** This is a missional, broad, timeless statement.

2. **O.** This is a very specific statement defining results to be achieved. It is time-bound and results would be measurable.

3. **O.** This is a specific statement that is time-bound with measurable results.

4. **G.** This is an aspiration with no time limit or specificity.

5. **O.** This is specific, measurable, and time-bound.

6. **G.** This is not measurable, has no time limit, and is not specific.

7. **G.** This is not measurable, has no time limit, and is not specific.

Exercise 2.3 (Pages 16–17)

1. *specific* and *measurable*

2. Use the acronym SMART, which stands for **s**pecific, **m**easurable, **a**ttainable, **r**esults-oriented, and **t**ime-bound.

3. *Stretch* means that future expectations described in objectives require greater extension or reach than is presently required.

4. Department X

5. reduce monthly backlog of orders processed from 30 percent to 15 percent

6. December 31 of this year

7. if backlog of orders processed is reduced to 15 percent by December 31 of this year

Exercise 2.6 (Pages 20–21)

1. A goal is a very broad, general statement. It is timeless and unconcerned with specific achievement.
   An objective is a measurable and specific statement of results to be achieved.

2. *a.* Performer (who)
   b. Action or performance (what)
   c. Time element (when)
   d. Evaluation method (how to measure achievement of objective)
   e. Place (where, if appropriate)

3. *c.* Outputs

4. activity trap

5. Your objective should be expressed in a manner similar to the following example: "Each department coordinator will increase the number of individuals pledging to the United Way from 40 percent to 50 percent over the next fiscal year."

6. Make sure your objective is specific, measurable, attainable, results-oriented, and time-bound. If it is, you have written a good objective. As you now know, writing specific, effective objectives is not an easy task. When you are satisfied with the final draft of your objective, submit it to your supervisor or ask a co-worker to read it and give you feedback. Remember, well-stated objectives should communicate exactly the same idea to the reader that the writer had in his or her mind. Most objectives can be improved and polished; therefore, the comments or questions from co-workers can be invaluable aids.

THE BUSINESS SKILLS EXPRESS SERIES

This growing series of books addresses a broad range of key business skills and topics to meet the needs of employees, human resource departments, and training consultants.

To obtain information about these and other Business Skills Express books, please call Business One IRWIN toll free at: 1-800-634-3966.